Quilted Bags
with Style

Quilted Bags
with Style

25 patchwork purses, totes, and bags

PHOTOGRAPHY BY TINO TEDALDI

Ellen Kharade

CICO BOOKS
LONDON NEW YORK

First published in 2005 by CICO Books as *Bags of Style*
This edition published in 2010 by CICO Books
an imprint of Ryland Peters & Small

20–21 Jockey's Fields   519 Broadway, 5th Floor
London WC1R 4BW   New York, NY 10012
www.cicobooks.com

10 9 8 7 6 5 4 3 2 1

Project designs copyright © Ellen Kharade, Emma Hardy and
Hilary More 2005, 2010
Design and photography © CICO Books 2005, 2010

A CIP catalog record for this book is available from the Library of
Congress and the British Library.

ISBN: 978-1-907030-55-0
(Previous ISBN: 978-1-904991-10-6)

Printed in China

Illustration: Kate Simunek
Editor: Alison Wormleighton
Photography: Tino Tedaldi
Design: Christine Wood
Additional styling: Denise Brock
Additional makes: Emma Hardy and Hilary More

contents

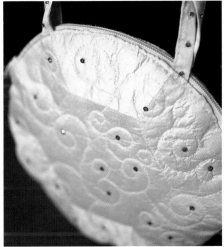

formal bags

A good selection of smart bags is an indispensable part of a wardrobe, particularly if they reflect your own personal style and favorite colors. There could be no better way to build up a truly individual collection of bags than to make them yourself, and patchwork offers a wealth of beautiful designs from which to choose. Using traditional techniques, you can create fresh, contemporary-looking bags in a wide range of fabrics. You will find a variety of styles in this chapter, ranging from the classic to the ultramodern. Although the techniques are quick and easy, the results are supremely stylish.

  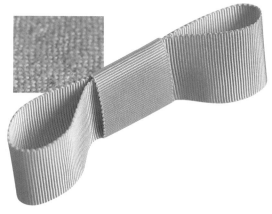

princess bag

This chic 1950s-inspired bag is made from squares of coordinating fabrics in shades of one color, to give it a fresh but distinctly sophisticated look. Grosgrain ribbon has been pleated to make a stylish trim around the top edge that matches the handles and simple bow. A glimpse of dark-color lining patterned with tiny polka-dots adds definition to the soft pastels.

The bag is 8¾ in. (22.5 cm) wide x 8 in. (20.5 cm) high (excluding handles) x 1¾ in. (4.5 cm) deep.

You will need:

◆ Scraps of four print fabrics in one color scheme, such as lime green

◆ ⅛ yd. (20 cm) of linen in a matching solid color

◆ Rotary cutter, acrylic ruler, cutting mat (optional)

◆ Matching sewing thread

◆ 10 x 20-in. (20 x 50-cm) piece of fusible interfacing

◆ ¼ yd. (20 cm) of print fabric in contrasting color, such as deep green polka dots, for lining

◆ 3⅛ yd. (3 m) of 1-in. (2.5-cm) grosgrain ribbon

◆ Fade-away marker pen (optional)

Coordinating fabrics in lime green with grosgrain trim create a retro look.

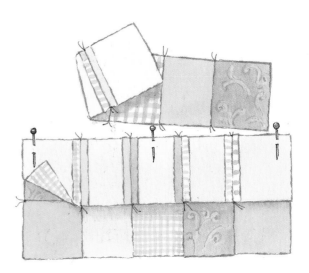

1 From the print fabrics and the linen, cut out forty 2¼-in. (5.5-cm) squares—about six to ten squares from each. A rotary cutter, acrylic ruler, and cutting mat are more accurate than scissors and will allow you to cut two layers of fabric at a time.

2 To piece the front and back, join five assorted solid and print squares into a row, right sides together and raw edges even, machine-stitching ¼-in. (5-mm) seams. Make seven more rows in the same way. Press all the seams open. Now pin two rows with right sides together and raw edges even, matching the seams; stitch a ¼-in. (5-mm) seam. Join two more rows to this section in the same way, to complete the front. Follow the same procedure to join the remaining four rows to make the back. Press the seams open.

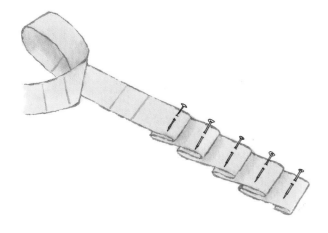

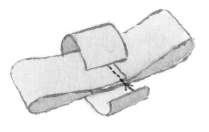

5 Using pins or a fade-away pen and starting at the left end of the ribbon, mark a line 1⅛ in. (3 cm) from the end and another line ½ in. (1.5 cm) further on. Now mark a third line a further 1⅛ in. (3 cm) along, followed by a fourth line another ½ in. (1.5 cm) along. Continue in the same way until you have marked 14 pairs of lines. Turn under the left end by ½ in. (1.5 cm), then pleat the ribbon by making an outer fold at the left line in each pair and an inner fold at the right line in each pair, pinning the pleats as you go. Check that the pleated ribbon is the right length to fit across the top of the bag exactly, and adjust the pleats as necessary. Cut the ribbon at the last mark, turning under ½ in. (1.5 cm) on the right end.

6 Repeat Step 5 to make a pleated ribbon for the back of the bag. Hand- or machine-baste the bottom edge of the pleated ribbons, removing the pins. Right sides together, pin and machine-baste the pleated ribbons to the top edge of the front and back on the right side, with the bottom edge of each ribbon even with the raw edge of the bag. For the bow, cut an 8½-in. (21.5-cm) length of ribbon, and overlap the ends by ¼ in. (5 mm) to form a loop, with the ends at the center. Machine-baste them together, through all three layers. Cut a 2½-in. (6.5 cm) length of ribbon, and wrap it over the center of the loop, overlapping the ends by ¼ in. (5 mm). Hand-sew the ends together, and then sew the ribbon to the loop.

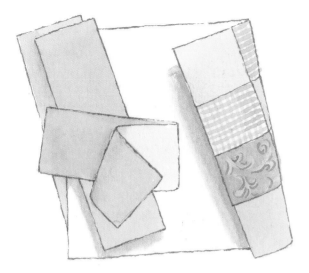

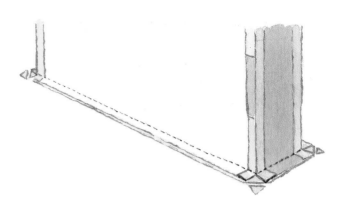

3 Cut two pieces of interfacing to the same size as the front and back—about 7½ x 9¼ in. (19 x 23.5 cm) each. Following the manufacturer's instructions, iron the interfacing to the wrong side of the patchwork front and back, making sure that the seam allowances are flat. From the linen, cut two pieces for the sides, each 2¼ in. (5.5 cm) wide and the same length as the height of the patchwork—about 7½ in. (19 cm), and one piece for the base, 2¼ in. (5.5 cm) wide and the same length as the width of the patchwork—about 9¼ in. (23.5 cm). From the lining fabric, cut pieces to the same size as the front, back, two sides, and base.

4 Right sides together and raw edges even, pin the sides to the front along the side edges, and machine-stitch ¼-in. (5-mm) seams, leaving the bottom ¼ in. (5 mm) of the seams unstitched. Join the remaining side edges of the sides to the back in the same way. Right sides together and raw edges even, pin the base to the bag using ¼-in. (5-mm) seams and allowing the unstitched portion of each side seam to open up at each corner, as shown. Adjust the size of the base or the width of the seams, if necessary, for a good fit. Machine-stitch, pivoting at the corners. Snip off the corners of the seam allowances, and press the seams open. Turn the bag right side out; press. Make the lining in the same way, but leave one long seam of the base unstitched.

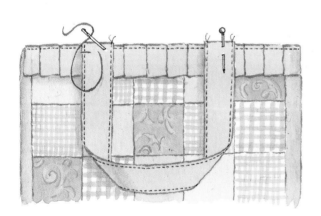

7 For the handles, cut two 24-in. (61-cm) lengths of ribbon and place one on top of the other. Pin and machine-stitch them together close to both side edges, then cut the length in half to make two double-thickness handles. Pin and hand-baste the ends of one handle to the right side of the front, on top of the pleated ribbon, 1¾ in. (4.5 cm) in from each side and with the ends even with the top edge of the bag. Pin and hand-baste the other handle to the back in the same way.

8 With the bag right side out and the lining wrong side out, slip the lining over the bag. With the top raw edges even and the side seams matching, pin the lining to the bag all the way around and machine-stitch a ¼-in. (5-mm) seam. Now pull the lining away from the bag, so it is right side out. Press the seam and press under ¼-in. (5-mm) seam allowances on the opening in the base of the lining. Slipstitch these edges together and push the lining inside the bag; press. Hand-sew the front side seam to the back side seam at the top of the bag, on the inside, as shown. Hand-sew the bow to the front of the bag near the top. Remove any visible basting.

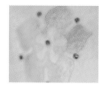
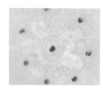
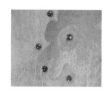

silk flower bag

This beautiful bag looks far more elaborate than it actually is. It features silk squares in different pale colors decorated with glass beads and hand-stamped gold flowers that are framed on the front with undecorated strips of silk in the same colors. In turn, the front is surrounded by sides, a back, a base, and strap handles in a deeper but similar shade of velvet. A satin lining provides a neat finish, and a button with a ribbon loop fastens the top.

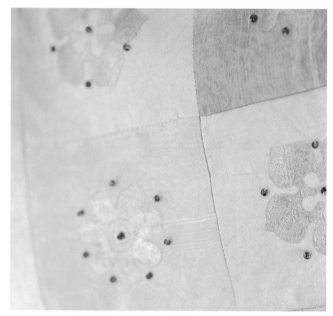

The bag is 9 in. (23 cm) wide x 9 in. (23 cm) high (excluding handles) x 1¾ in. (4.5 cm) deep.

You will need:

◆ ¼ yd. (20 cm), in total, of silk in at least four colors, such as pale pink, mid pink, peach, and orange

◆ ⅓ yd. (30 cm) of velvet in a deeper tone, such as deep pink

◆ ⅓ yd. (30 cm) of satin fabric in same color as velvet, for the lining

◆ Rotary cutter, acrylic ruler, cutting mat (optional)

◆ Piece of sponge, gold fabric paint, fine artist's paintbrush

◆ Flower stamps in two designs

◆ Matching sewing thread

◆ 10-in. (26-cm) square of fusible interfacing

◆ 30 small glass beads in a harmonizing color, such as lilac

◆ ⅓ yd. (30 cm) of narrow ribbon in a harmonizing color, such as pink

◆ One button and one sequin in a color to match ribbon

Deep pink velvet sets off pale pink and peach silk stamped with gold.

1 From the silks, cut out two 3½-in. (8.5-cm) squares from each of two colors (or all four squares can be different colors), two 2¼ x 6½-in. (6 x 16-cm) strips from the third color, and two 2¼ x 10-in. (6 x 26-cm) strips from the fourth, all for the front. From the velvet, cut out a 10-in. (26-cm) square for the back and three 2¾ x 10-in. (7.5 x 26-cm) strips for the sides and base. From the satin, cut out two 10-in. (26-cm) squares and three 10 x 2¾-in. (7.5 x 26-cm) strips. A rotary cutter, acrylic ruler, and cutting mat are more accurate than scissors and will allow you to cut two layers of silk or satin at once. (The velvet should be cut one layer at a time.)

2 Place the pieces for the front on newspaper or a sheet of plastic to protect your work surface. Dip the piece of sponge in a little of the paint, and then lightly dab the paint onto one of the stamps. Press the stamp onto the center of one silk square, and carefully lift it away. Use a fine paint-brush and a little more paint to touch up any areas that look thin. Use the same stamp for the diagonally opposite patch, and the second stamp for the other two silk patches. Let it dry. Place a clean cloth over the motif and iron to fix the design, following the paint manufacturer's instructions.

5 If desired, make a small dart in each side at the top, to give the bag some shape. Press under ½ in. (1.5-cm) all around the top edge of the bag.

6 For the handles, cut two 1½ x 20-in. (4 x 50-cm) strips of velvet. Fold one long edge of one strip into the center, wrong sides together, and hand-baste in place. Repeat for the other long edge of the strip. Turn in ¼ in. (5 mm) at each end, and then fold the strip in half lengthwise, enclosing all the raw edges. Pin and machine-stitch along the long edge and both ends. Make the second handle in the same way. Pin and hand-baste the ends of one handle to the wrong side of the front, and the ends of the other to the wrong side of the back, positioning all four ends the same distance from the sides.

3 To piece the front, pin and machine-stitch the pieces, right sides together and raw edges even, using ¼-in. (5-mm) seams and pressing the seams open as you go, working in the following sequence: join the top two silk squares, do the same for the bottom two silk squares, then stitch these two sections together, matching the seams. Stitch one of the shorter silk strips to each side, and then the two longer silk strips to the top and bottom. From the interfacing, cut out a 10-in. (26-cm) square. Following the manufacturer's instructions, iron the interfacing to the wrong side of the patchwork, making sure that the seam allowances are flat. Decorate the stamped flowers by hand-sewing glass beads to the centers and around the edges.

4 Right sides together and raw edges even, pin the long edges of the two velvet strips for the sides to the side edges of the front. Machine-stitch ½-in. (1.5-cm) seams, leaving the bottom ½ in. (1.5-cm) of the seams unstitched. Join the remaining long edges of the sides to the side edges of the velvet back in the same way. Right sides together and raw edges even, pin the base to the bag, using ½-in. (1.5-cm) seams and allowing the unstitched portion of each side seam to open up at each corner, as shown. Adjust the size of the base or the width of the seams, if necessary, for a good fit. Machine-stitch, pivoting at the corners. Snip off the corners of the seam allowances, and press the seams open.

7 Make the lining from the satin pieces in the same way as for the bag, Steps 4 and 5. Turn the bag right side out. With the lining wrong side out, push it into the bag, matching the side seams. Carefully pin the lining to the bag around the top. Machine-stitch close to the edge, catching in the carriers and tab at the same time. Remove the basting. To give the handles extra strength, stitch again parallel to the previous stitching, being sure to stitch over the ends of the handles.

8 Make a loop with the narrow ribbon and hand-sew it to the wrong side of the back at the center. Sew a button to the right side of the front, embellishing it with a sequin sewn to its center, and then secure the bag by looping the ribbon over the button.

 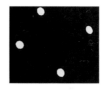 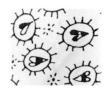 

modern black and white bag

Made from random-width patches of black-and-white prints, this stylish bag goes equally well with white sportswear or black evening wear, as well as with stripes or solid colors, such as red. The round black handles echo both the shape of the bag and the color theme, while the diagonal arrangement of the patches adds to the dynamic feel. All the sewing is quick and easy, because the patches, which are all rectangles of the same length, are simply sewn together into long strips, which are joined without the need for any seam matching.

The bag is 14½ in. (35.5 cm) in diameter (excluding handles).

You will need:

◆ ⅛ yd. (10 cm) each of six fabrics in black-and-white prints

◆ ¼ yd. (20 cm) of black fabric

◆ Rotary cutter, acrylic ruler, cutting mat (optional)

◆ Matching sewing thread

◆ ½ yd. (40 cm) of fusible interfacing

◆ Paper for pattern

◆ 12-in. (30 cm) length of string

◆ Pair of 6-in. (15-cm)-wide round black handles

◆ 16 round pearl buttons

◆ ½ yd. (40 cm) of white or black fabric, for lining

Restricting the bag's colors to black and white creates an ultramodern look.

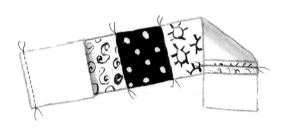

1 From each of the seven fabrics, cut a strip 3½ in. (8.5 cm) wide and about 1 yd. (1 m) long. Now cut the strips into pieces varying from about 1½ in. to 4 in. (4 cm to 10 cm) wide, to make about 80 pieces that are all the same length but are different widths. The solid-black pieces will look best if they are no more than about 2 in. (5 cm) wide. A rotary cutter, acrylic ruler, and cutting mat are more accurate than scissors and will allow you to cut two layers of fabric at a time.

2 Pin one piece to a second one in a different fabric along one side edge, right sides together and raw edges even, and machine-stitch a ¼-in. (5 mm) seam. Repeat to join more pieces together until you have a row of about seven to nine pieces, with a total width of at least 15½ in. (38.5 cm), and including a variety of fabrics and widths. Make nine more rows in the same way. Press the seams open.

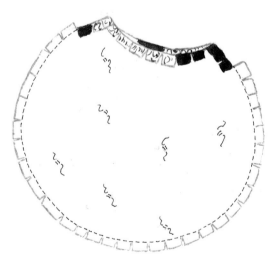

5 Place one pieced section so the corner is at the top, like a diamond, and the rows of patches are on the diagonal. Pin the pattern to it with the cutout curve at the top. Make sure the fabric extends up to or beyond the edge of the pattern all the way around. Cut out the pieced shape. Repeat for the other patchwork square. Hand-sew buttons to the patchwork seamlines in a regular pattern.

6 Right sides together and raw edges even, pin the two pieced sections together so the cutout areas are on top of each other. Machine-stitch a ½-in. (1.5-cm) seam around the edge, leaving the curved top unstitched. Clip into the seam allowances of the seam, and press it open. Press under ½ in. (1.5 cm) on the top edges, clipping into the seam allowances. Using the pattern, cut out two pieces of the lining fabric, and make the lining in the same way. Turn the bag right side out, and press.

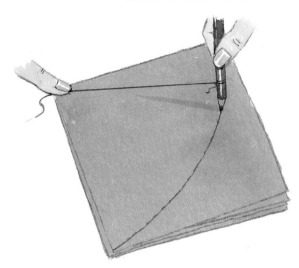

3 Right sides together and raw edges even, pin one row to another, trying to avoid placing pieces from the same fabric next to each other. Machine-stitch a ¼-in. (5 mm) seam. Now join three more rows to this section in the same way, so that the pieced section is roughly square and the light and dark tones are fairly balanced. It doesn't matter if the ends of the rows are not quite even. Join the remaining five rows in the same way to form another square. Press the seams open. Cut out two squares of fusible interfacing the same size as each pieced section. Following the manufacturer's instructions, iron the interfacing to the wrong side of each section, making sure that the seam allowances are flat.

4 To make a circular paper pattern, cut out a square of paper exactly the same size as the patchwork section at its narrowest point, about 15½ in. (38.5 cm) across. Fold the paper in fourths. Tie one end of the string to a pencil, and hold the other end at the folded corner of the square (the center when it is unfolded) so you can use them like a compass. Adjust the string until the pencil reaches to the edge of the paper with the string taut, then draw a quarter-circle. Cut this out and unfold it—the pattern should be a circle with a diameter of 15½ in (38.5 cm). Using one handle as a guide, cut a shallow arc out of the edge of the pattern.

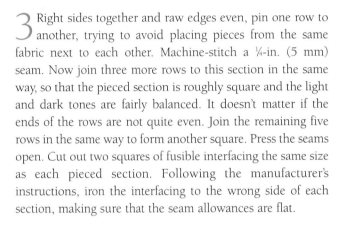

7 For the carriers, cut out a 2¼ x 21-in. (6 x 54-cm) strip from the black fabric. Fold it in half lengthwise, right sides together, and then pin and machine-stitch a ¼-in. (5-mm) seam down the long edge. Attach a safety pin to one end. Thread the safety pin through the tube of fabric, pulling it through to turn the fabric right side out. Press it flat, and then cut it into six 3½-in. (9-cm) carriers.

8 Wrap one carrier over one handle, and hand-baste the ends together. Repeat for two more carriers. Pin the ends of one to the inside of the front at the top, 1 in. (2.5 cm) from the side seam. Pin another carrier 1 in. (2.5 cm) from the other side, and a third in the center. Wrap the remaining three over the second handle; hand-baste; and pin in the same positions on the back. Machine-baste all six carriers. With the lining wrong side out, push it into the bag, matching the side seams, and pin it around the top. Machine-stitch close to the edge, catching in the carriers at the same time. Remove the basting.

pyramid bag

Three floral prints and a plaid, all in harmonizing colors, are used for the pieces making up this striking bag. Rectangles of the same width, but of random lengths, are sewn together into strips. The sides of the strips are then cut at angles before being stitched together, creating the bag's tapered shape. At the top, a solid-color band, trimmed with a matching ribbon and discreetly decorated with small pearl buttons, provides a crisp finish to the patchwork, complemented by the curve of the handles.

The bag is about 12 in. (31 cm) wide x 13 in. (34.5 cm) high (excluding handles).

You will need:

◆ ¼ yd. (20 cm) each of three print fabrics and ⅔ yd. (60 cm) of a fourth print, all in coordinating colors

◆ Rotary cutter, acrylic ruler, cutting mat (optional)

◆ Matching sewing thread

◆ Paper for patterns

◆ ⅛ yd. (10 cm) of fabric in a solid color to match others

◆ 1 yd. (1 m) of ½-in. (1-cm)-wide matching velvet ribbon

◆ ½ yd. (50 cm) of fusible interfacing

◆ ½ yd. (50 cm) of ¾-in. (1-cm)-wide matching satin ribbon

◆ Pair of 6-in. (15-cm)-wide curved handles

◆ Snap fastener

◆ 10 round pearl buttons

Tortoiseshell-effect handles set off a burgundy color theme.

1 From each of the four print fabrics, cut a strip 4¼ in. (11 cm) wide and about 1 yd. (1 m) long. Now cut the strips into pieces varying from about 1½ in. to 3½ in. (4 cm to 9 cm) long, to make about 50 pieces that are all the same width but are different lengths. A rotary cutter, acrylic ruler, and cutting mat are more accurate than scissors and will allow you to cut two layers of fabric at a time.

2 Pin the bottom edge of one piece to the top edge of a piece in a different fabric, right sides together and raw edges even, and machine-stitch a ¼-in. (5-mm) seam. Repeat to join more pieces together until you have a vertical row of about five to seven patches, with a total length of 12½ in. (33 cm), and including a variety of fabrics and sizes. Make seven more vertical rows in the same way. Press the seams open.

5 Cut two strips of solid-color fabric 2¼ in. (5.5 cm) wide and as long as the width of the top edge of the front— about 8½ in. (22 cm). Right sides together and raw edges even, pin the long edge of one strip to the top edge of the front; machine-stitch a ¼-in. (5-mm) seam. Join the other strip to the back in the same way. Pin and topstitch velvet ribbon to the strip about ¼ in. (1 cm) above the lower edge of the strip, on both the front and back. Cut two pieces of interfacing and two pieces of the fourth fabric for the lining, all to the same size as the front and back. Following the manufacturer's instructions, iron the interfacing to the wrong side of the patchwork front and back, making sure that the seam allowances are flat.

6 Pin the front to the back, right sides together and raw edges even, and machine-stitch a ½-in. (1-cm) seam around the sides and bottom, pivoting at the bottom corners. Snip off the corners of the seam allowances and press open the seams. Press under a ½-in. (1.5-cm) hem along the top raw edges. Make the lining from the two lining pieces in the same way.

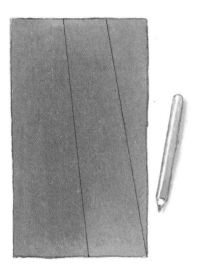

3 To make the two patterns, cut a paper rectangle 7¼ in. (18.5 cm) wide x 12½ in. (33 cm) long. At the top, mark points 3 in. (7.5 cm) from the left edge and 2¼ in. (6 cm) from the right edge. At the bottom, mark a point 3 in. (7.5 cm) from the right edge. Draw a straight line between the left-hand mark at the top and the mark at the bottom. Draw a second line between the right-hand mark at the top and the bottom right corner. Now cut along both these lines and discard the triangle on the right.

4 Decide where each vertical row will be positioned on the front and back, and, starting from the left, label the front vertical rows 1 to 4 and the back ones (again starting from the left) 5 to 8. Pin the wider pattern to the right side of row 3 and cut out the shape. Repeat for row 7, then turn the pattern over and use it to cut out rows 2 and 6. With the other pattern, cut out rows 4 and 8, then turn it over and cut out rows 1 and 5. Now join the four rows of the front in the correct order, pinning and machine-stitching the pieces, right sides together and raw edges even, using ¼-in. (5 mm) seams. Repeat for the back. Press the seams open.

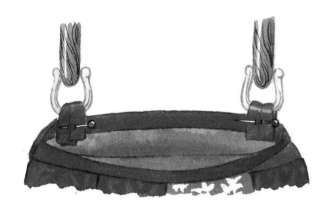

7 For the handle carriers, cut eight 2-in. (5-cm) lengths of satin ribbon, and thread these through the rings at the ends of the handles. Baste the ends together. Using the handles as a guide to positioning, pin and then baste these carriers to the top edge of the bag front and back, on the wrong side. For the tab, cut two 1¾ x 2½-in. (4.5 x 6.5-cm) rectangles from one of the patterned fabrics. Pin one to the other around the edges, right sides together and raw edges even. Stitch a ¼-in. (5-mm) seam down each side, tapering to a point at one end. Snip off the corners of the seam allowances at the bottom. Turn right side out and press. Pin and baste the tab to the top edge of the bag back, centering it on the wrong side.

8 Turn the bag right side out. With the lining wrong side out, push it into the bag, matching the side seams. Carefully pin the lining to the bag around the top. Machine-stitch close to the edge, catching in the carriers and the tab at the same time. Remove the basting. Hand-sew the "ball" of the snap to the underside of the tab and the "socket" of the snap to the right side of the bag near the top, so that they align exactly. Hand-sew the buttons to the ribbon on the front and back, and sew one to the outside of the tab so it is in line with those on the ribbon.

checkerboard heart bag

Heart motifs decorate the checkerboard-pattern front of this stylish bag made from felted wool. The curvy lines of the hearts contrast with the straight lines of the grid pattern, while the muted colors in combination with the sensible, sturdy shape and upstanding handles provide a sophisticated counterbalance to the folk-art motifs. A row of dark seed pearls adds definition. Inside the bag, the lining has a useful pocket, which is decorated with glass beads.

The bag is 9½ in. (26.5 cm) wide x 7½ in. (21 cm) high (excluding handles) x 3½ in. (11 cm) deep.

You will need:

◆ Paper and stiff cardstock for patterns

◆ ⅓ yd. (30 cm), in total, of felted wool in three similar colors, such as green, turquoise, and blue

◆ ⅓ yd. (30 cm) of cotton fabric in a coordinating color, such as pale blue, for lining

◆ Matching sewing thread

◆ Fine-point marker pen and fabric glue

◆ 5 x 32-in. (12 x 80-cm) piece of artist's plastic mesh (available from craft stores)

◆ 18 glass beads and 22 seed pearls or sequins

Cool, harmonious colors lend elegance to a lighthearted design.

1 Enlarge and transfer the templates from page 120 onto paper, then cut out the patterns. From the first color, cut out one back using the pattern, one 5 x 10¾-in. (12 x 27.5-cm) rectangle for the base, and one 2 x 31½-in. (5 x 80-cm) strip for handles. From the second color, cut out two sides using the pattern. From all three colors, use the patterns to cut out the nine pieces for the front, making sure that adjacent pieces are not in the same color and that the central and corner pieces are not in the first color. From the lining fabric, cut out two pieces from the back pattern (one will be used for the lining front), two sides using the side pattern, and a 5 x 10¾-in. (12 x 27.5-cm) base.

2 Use the heart template to make a pattern from cardstock. With the marker pen, draw around the heart pattern on the center and corner pieces for the front, placing the pattern in the center of each. Using very sharp scissors, carefully cut out the shapes. Seal the edges of the hearts with fabric glue on the wrong side and allow to dry.

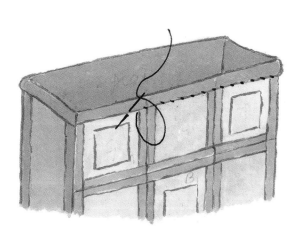

5 Press under ¼ in. (5 mm) all around the top edge of the bag, hand-sew neatly in place, and then turn the bag right side out. Cut out two strips of plastic mesh, one measuring 4½ x 10¼ in. (11 x 26.5 cm) and the other ¾ x 31½ in. (2 x 80 cm), and place the shorter one in the bottom of the bag, hand-sewing the corners to the inside of the bag.

6 Press under ¼ in. (5 mm) on the long edges of the long fabric strip. Wrap the strip around the long mesh strip, right side out, and slipstitch the folded edges together. Cut the fabric-enclosed mesh in half, and hand-sew the ends of one of these handles to the wrong side of the front, and the ends of the other to the wrong side of the back, positioning all four ends the same distance from the sides.

3 To piece the front, join the patches into rows of three, pinning and machine-stitching them with right sides together and raw edges even, using ¼-in. (5-mm) seams and pressing the seams open as you go. Matching the seamlines, join the three rows in the same way. From the first color, cut out five squares slightly larger than the heart motif, and glue one square to the back of each heart cutout. Let it dry for at least two hours.

4 Right sides together and raw edges even, pin the sides to the front along the side edges and machine-stitch ¼-in. (5-mm) seams, leaving the bottom ¼ in. (5 mm) of the seams unstitched. Join the remaining side edges of the sides to the back in the same way. Right sides together and raw edges even, pin the base to the bag using ¼-in. (5-mm) seams and allowing the unstitched portion of each side seam to open up at each corner, as shown. Adjust the size of the base or the width of the seams, if necessary, for a good fit. Machine-stitch, pivoting at the corners. Snip off the corners of the seam allowances, and press the seams open.

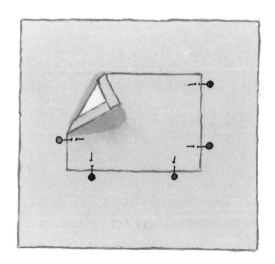

7 From the lining fabric, cut out a 4 x 5-in. (10 x 13 cm) rectangle for a pocket. Press under ½ in. (1 cm) on all four edges. Topstitch one long edge. With this edge at the top, pin the pocket to the right side of the lining back, 1¾ in. (4.5 cm) from the top. Topstitch the pocket down one side, along the bottom, and up the other side. Topstitch vertically down the center. Decorate the edges of the pocket with a row of beads.

8 Make up the lining as in Step 4, then press under ¼ in. (5 mm) around the top edge. With the lining wrong side out, push the lining inside the bag, matching the side seams. Pin the lining to the bag around the top. Machine-stitch close to the edge, catching in the handles at the same time. Hand-sew seed pearls or sequins along the top of the bag at the front.

yo-yo bag

Fabric circles gathered up to form rosettes, known as yo-yos among quilters, create a delightful three-dimensional effect on this bag. Sewn together and then to the central panel, they are very quick to make. The use of plaids for the yo-yos on the bag was inspired by Scottish tam-o'-shanters, but checked or striped fabrics would work particularly well, too. With lighter-colored fabrics you could embroider cross stitches or French knots on each yo-yo. Inside the bag is a handy pocket.

The bag is 11¼ in. (28.5 cm) wide x 9¼ in. (23.5 cm) high (excluding handles) x 1¾ in. (4.5 cm) deep.

You will need:

◆ Compass and paper for pattern

◆ ¼ yd. (20 cm) each of non-bulky fabric such as cotton in two coordinating plaids

◆ ⅓ yd. (30 cm) of non-bulky fabric such as cotton in a third coordinating plaid

◆ Matching quilting thread and sewing thread

◆ ¼ yd. (20 cm) of a fabric in a coordinating solid color, such as peach

◆ ½ yd. (50 cm) of a fabric in a second coordinating solid color, such as green

◆ Rotary cutter, acrylic ruler, cutting mat (optional)

◆ ⅓ yd. (30 cm) of fusible interfacing

◆ 2 x 12-in. (5 x 30-cm) piece of artist's plastic mesh (available from craft stores)

A single small pattern in coordinating colors is best for the yo-yos on this bag.

1 Using a compass, draw a circle with a diameter of 3¾ in. (9.5 cm) on a piece of paper, and cut it out. Use this pattern to cut out eight circles from each of the three plaid fabrics. Turn under ¼ in. (5 mm) around the edge of each circle, and finger-press. Knot a piece of quilting thread, and hand-sew even running stitches all around the hemmed edge of one circle, overlapping the first and last stitches. Pull the ends to gather up the fabric tightly. Make several backstitches to secure the thread before cutting it. Do the same for the other 23 circles.

2 With the hole in the center of each yo-yo, press them gently beneath a damp towel, using a steam iron. Place two yo-yos together with the holes facing outward, and join them with several hand-stitches at one edge. Continue sewing them together until you have six rows of four yo-yos each. Now sew three rows together in the same way, with several hand-stitches joining adjacent yo-yos; these will go on the front of the bag. Repeat to sew three more rows together, for the back of the bag.

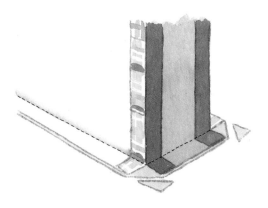

5 From the other solid-color fabric, cut three 10¼ x 12¼-in. (26.5 x 31.5-cm) rectangles (for the back and the lining front and back), four 2¾ x 10¼-in. (7.5 x 26.5-cm) strips (for the sides and the lining sides), two 2¾ x 12¼-in. (7.5 x 31.5-cm) strips (for the base and the lining base), and two 3 x 16-in. (7.5 x 40-cm) strips (for the handles). If you would like a pocket inside the bag, also cut a 5½ x 7½-in. (14 x 19-cm) rectangle from the third plaid fabric, press under ¼ in. (5 mm) on each edge, and stitch across one long edge. Pin the pocket centrally to one lining piece. Topstitch along the side and bottom edges and also from the top edge to the bottom edge of the pocket to create two compartments.

6 Right sides together and raw edges even, pin the bag sides to the bag front along the side edges, and machine-stitch ½-in. (1.5-cm) seams, leaving the bottom ½ in. (1.5 cm) of the seams unstitched. Join the remaining side edges of the sides to the bag back in the same way. Right sides together and raw edges even, pin the base to the bag using ½-in. (1.5-cm) seams and allowing the unstitched portion of each side seam to open up at each corner, as shown. Adjust the size of the base or the width of the seams, if necessary, for a good fit. Machine-stitch, pivoting at the corners. Snip off the corners of the seam allowances, and press the seams open. Press under ½ in. (1.5 cm) around the top edge. Make the lining in the same way.

3 From one solid-color fabric, cut two 5¾ x 7¾-in. (14.5 x 19.5-cm) rectangles. From the third plaid fabric, cut four 2¾ x 5¾-in. (8.5 x 14.5-cm) strips and four 2¾ x 12¼-in. (8.5 x 31.5-cm) strips. A rotary cutter, acrylic ruler, and cutting mat are more accurate than scissors and will allow you to cut two layers of fabric at a time. Right sides together and raw edges even, pin a short plaid strip to each short edge of the solid-color rectangle. Machine-stitch ¼-in. (5-mm) seams. Press the seams open. Now join a long strip to the top and another to the bottom of the rectangle in the same way. Repeat for the remaining pieces.

4 Cut out two 10¼ x 12¼-in. (26.5 x 31.5-cm) rectangles of fusible interfacing. Following the manufacturer's instructions, iron the interfacing to the wrong side of each pieced section, making sure that the seam allowances are flat. Hand-sew the yo-yos to the center rectangle of each pieced section using a few tiny stitches at the edge of each yo-yo.

7 Cut a 1¾ x 11¼-in. (4.5 x 28.5-cm) rectangle of plastic mesh (adjusting the size to fit the base if you adjusted that in Step 6). Hand-sew it to the wrong side of the base using a few stitches at each side. For the handles, fold one long edge of one strip into the center, wrong sides together. Repeat for the other long edge of the strip, and then fold the strip in half lengthwise, enclosing the raw edges. Press. Pin and machine-stitch along the long edge. Make the second handle in the same way. Pin and hand-baste the ends of one handle to the wrong side of the front, and the ends of the other handle to the wrong side of the back. The center of each end should be in line with the edge of the central rectangle on the front and back.

8 Turn the bag right side out, and press. With the lining wrong side out, push it into the bag, matching the side seams. Carefully pin the lining to the bag around the top. Machine-stitch close to the edge, catching in the ends of the handles at the same time. Remove the basting.

shoppers and totes

Totes are the most hard-working of all types of bags, but the beautiful patchwork designs in this chapter prove that they can also be fashionable. Whether you want an elegant silk and velvet tote, a cheerful carryall in bright pastel cottons with bamboo handles, a girl's overnight bag, or a variety of stylish totes in geometric prints, there are plenty of inspiring projects from which to choose. Ranging from the compact to the spacious, they will prove ideal traveling companions for anything from a trip to the grocery store to a day at the beach.

flower and striped tote

A bold, modern floral fabric is teamed with a coordinating stripe to great effect to make this contemporary-looking patchwork tote. Use solid colors alongside the prints so that the pattern does not overpower the style. To make a handy, practical bag suitable for everyday use, line it with batting for protection and strength. Here, the layers are joined together with simple ditch-quilting, where stitching along the patchwork seams holds the structure in place.

The tote is 22 in. (56 cm) wide x 14 in. (36 cm) high (excluding handles).

You will need:

◆ ⅓ yd. (30 cm) each of floral print and striped fabric

◆ 1⅛ yd. (1 m), in total, of two solid-color fabrics

◆ Rotary cutter, acrylic ruler, cutting mat (optional)

◆ Matching sewing thread

◆ ⅔ yd. (60 cm) of lightweight polyester batting

Flowers and stripes make a perfect summer style combination.

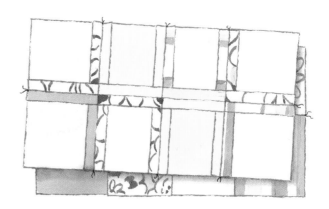

1 For the front, cut out eight 6-in. (15-cm) squares of different fabrics, such as three floral, two striped, and three solid-color. A rotary cutter, acrylic ruler, and cutting mat are more accurate than scissors and will allow you to cut two layers of fabric at a time. Arrange the pieces in a pleasing pattern. Right sides together and raw edges even, pin the top four squares together in a row. Machine-stitch ¼-in. (5-mm) seams and press the seams open. Repeat for the bottom row of squares.

2 Right sides together and raw edges even, pin the two rows together, matching the seams, to make a panel of eight squares. Machine-stitch ¼-in. (5-mm) seams; press the seams open. Repeat Steps 1 and 2 to make the back of the bag.

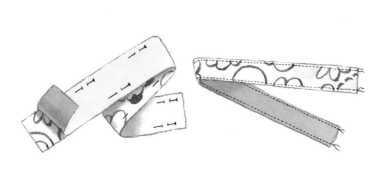

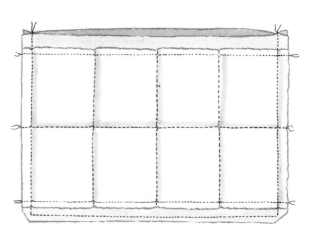

5 For the straps, cut four 1½ x 25-in. (4 x 63-cm) strips of fabric, two in floral and two in solid-color fabric. Right sides together, pin a floral strip to a solid strip along the long edges and machine-stitch ¼-in. (5-mm) seams. Turn the strap right side out by fastening a safety pin to a layer of fabric at one end of the strap and threading it through to the other end. Press the strap flat and topstitch along each long edge. Repeat to make a second strap from the other two strips of fabric.

6 Right sides together and raw edges even, pin the front and back pieces together along the side and bottom edges. Machine-stitch a ¼-in. (5-mm) seam, pivoting at the corners. Snip off the corners of the seam allowance at the bottom, turn the bag right side out, and press. For the lining, cut two 14¾ x 22½-in. (37 x 57-cm) pieces of solid-colored fabric. Right sides together and raw edges even, pin and machine-stitch a ¼-in. (5-mm) seam along each short edge. Press the seams open.

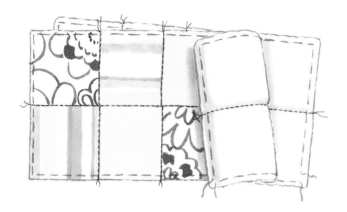

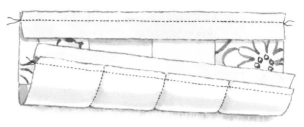

3 Cut two pieces of batting to the same size as the front and back—about 11½ x 22½ in. (29 x 57 cm). Lay a patchwork panel over one piece, and pin and baste the two layers together. Repeat with the other patchwork panel and the second piece of batting. Now "ditch-quilt" the layers by machine-stitching over the seams. Repeat with the other patchwork panel and the second piece of batting. Remove the basting.

4 Cut four 2 x 22½-in. (5 x 57-cm) solid-color strips for the top and bottom edging of the front and back. Pin one strip along the top edge of one patchwork panel, and one strip along the bottom of the panel; machine-stitch ¼-in. (5-mm) seams. Press open the seams. Repeat for the second patchwork panel and the remaining strips.

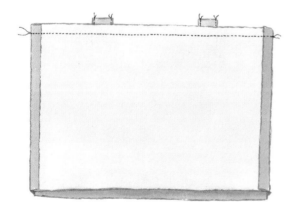

7 Right sides together, pull the lining over the bag, with the raw edges even at the top. Place one handle on the front of the bag, sandwiched between the patchwork and lining, with the ends ¼ in. (5 mm) above the raw edge of the bag; the outside edges of the handle should be aligned with the seamline between the two outer pieces (see photo). Baste the ends in place. Repeat for the other handle. Pin the lining to the bag around the top. Machine-stitch a ¼-in. (5-mm) seam all the way around. Turn the lining right side out, press under ¼ in. (5 mm) on the raw edges, and slipstitch them together. Push the lining inside the bag. Press. Remove any visible basting.

summertime tote

Fresh colors and simple patterns are ideal for this cheerful tote that features the ever-popular patchwork design known as flying geese. A small sprigged cotton is used for the five triangles that make up each block on the front, with a matching gingham for the smaller triangles framing the larger ones. Narrow sashing strips in the same sprigged print separate the three flying-geese blocks, while a polka-dot cotton surrounds them. The back is quick and easy to make up, simply comprising rectangles in the three fabrics. The handles are made from strips of the sprigged print.

The bag is 15½ in. (39.5 cm) wide x 17 in. (43 cm) high (excluding handles).

You will need:

◆ ½ yd. (50 cm) of a print fabric in a summery color such as sky blue and white

◆ Rotary cutter, acrylic ruler, cutting mat (optional)

◆ ⅓ yd. (30 cm) of a small-check gingham in the same color

◆ ½ yd. (50 cm) of a polka-dot fabric in the same color

◆ Matching sewing thread

◆ Paper for pattern

◆ ½ yd. (50 cm) of fusible interfacing

◆ ½ yd. (50 cm) of white fabric, for lining

◆ ⅔ yd. (60 cm) of narrow ribbon in the same color as print fabric

◆ Two large glass beads

Sky blue is the perfect color for a bag with a flying-geese design.

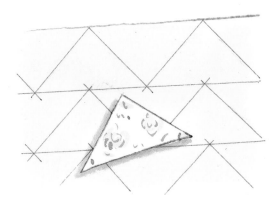

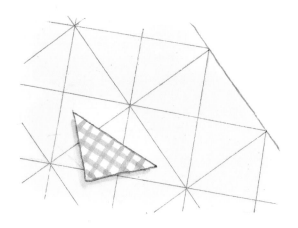

1 On the wrong side of the print fabric, draw lines 2¼ in. (5.5 cm) apart on the straight grain until you have marked out strips totaling about 2 yd. (170 cm) in length. On alternate lines mark a point 2¼ in. (5.5 cm) from one edge and then further points 4½ in. (11 cm) apart. On the remaining lines, mark the first point 4½ in. (11 cm) from the edge and other points 4½ in. (11 cm) apart. Draw straight lines between the points in a zigzag pattern and then cut along the lines, until you have 15 triangles. A rotary cutter, acrylic ruler, and cutting mat are more accurate than scissors and will allow you to cut two layers of fabric at a time.

2 On the wrong side of the gingham, draw a grid of lines 2½ in. (6 cm) apart on the bias (diagonal), until you have marked out about 15 squares. Now draw a zigzag pattern connecting alternate points on adjacent lines. Cut along the lines, to make 30 smaller triangles. Right sides together and raw edges even, pin the long edge of one small triangle to one of the short edges of a large triangle, and machine-stitch a ¼-in. (5-mm) seam. Join a second small triangle to the other short edge of the large triangle in the same way, forming a rectangle. Repeat until you have 15 rectangles. Press the seams open and trim off the corners of the seam allowances, even with the raw edges.

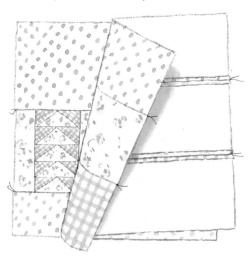

5 From the polka-dot fabric, cut two rectangles to the width of the pieced section—about 16½ in. (42.5 cm)— the first one 7½ in. (18 cm) deep and the other 3 in. (7.5 cm) deep. Pin the first to the top of the pieced section and the second to the bottom along the long edges, right sides together and raw edges even. Stitch ¼-in. (5-mm) seams. This will be the front. For the back, cut three rectangles to the same width as the front. The first, from the polka-dot fabric, should be 5 in. (13 cm) deep and the second, from the print, 7 in. (18 cm) deep. The third, from the gingham should be equal to the depth of the front less 11 in. (29 cm), or about 7 in. (17 cm). Join these in the same way as for the front.

6 Enlarge and transfer the template from page 121 onto paper, then cut out the pattern. For the front of the bag, pin the pattern to the center of the pieced section and cut out the shape. Repeat for the back. Also use the pattern to cut out two pieces of fusible interfacing and two pieces of lining fabric. Following the manufacturer's instructions, iron the interfacing to the wrong side of the front and back, making sure that the seam allowances are flat. Right sides together and raw edges even, pin the front to the back around the sides and bottom. Machine-stitch a ½-in. (1.5-cm) seam. Clip into the seam allowances on the curves. Press the seam open and press under a ½-in. (1.5-cm) hem along the top raw edges. Make the lining from the two lining pieces in the same way.

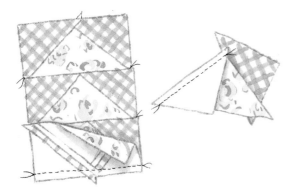

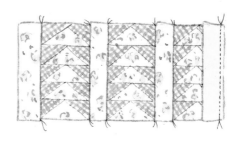

3 Right sides together and raw edges even, pin the bottom edge of one pieced rectangle to the top edge of another, being careful to stitch just through the point of the triangle. Machine-stitch a ¼-in. (5-mm) seam. Join three more pieced rectangles to these two in the same way. Now stitch five more pieced rectangles together in the same way, and then join the last five, so that you have three vertical rows in all. Press the seams open.

4 From the print fabric, cut four strips 2 in. (5 cm) wide and as long as the height of the pieced sections—about 8½ in. (22.5 cm). Join the long edges of the strips to those of the pieced sections, right sides together and raw edges even, with the strips and vertical rows alternating. Machine-stitch ¼-in. (5-mm) seams, being careful to stitch through the point of each triangle. Press the seams open.

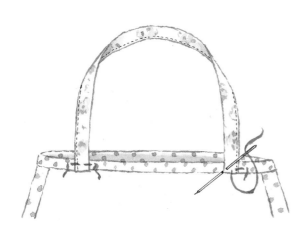

7 For the handles, cut two 3 x 16-in. (7.5 x 41-cm) strips of the print fabric. Fold one long edge of one strip into the center, wrong sides together. Repeat for the other long edge of the strip, and then fold the strip in half lengthwise, enclosing the raw edges. Press. Pin and machine-stitch along the long edge. Make the second handle in the same way. Pin and hand-baste the ends of one handle to the wrong side of the front and the ends of the other to the wrong side of the back, positioning the center of each 2 in. (5 cm) from the sides.

8 Turn the bag right side out and press. With the lining wrong side out, push it into the bag, matching the side seams. Carefully pin the lining to the bag around the top. Machine-stitch close to the edge, catching in the ends of the handles at the same time. Remove the basting. Cut two 11-in. (28-cm) lengths of ribbon, and hand-sew the center of each to the top edge of the bag at the side seam. Hand-sew a bead on top of each ribbon.

silk and velvet tote

Subtly different tones of one color allow the eye to focus on the pattern and texture of this beautiful tote. On both the front and the back, strips and squares of solid-color silk and velvet contrast with squares cut from fabrics in several small-scale patterns, while velvet straps add rich texture. The bag is flat, with the back and front simply stitched together, but a shaped outline and a patterned lining add interest. A line of matching buttons at front and back adds further subtle detail.

The bag is 22 in. (53 cm) wide x 15¼ in. (35.5 cm) high (excluding handles).

You will need:

◆ Scraps of four print fabrics, all in the same color scheme, such as purple

◆ ½ yd. (40 cm) each of solid-colored silk and velvet in same color as prints

◆ Rotary cutter, acrylic ruler, cutting mat (optional)

◆ Matching sewing thread

◆ Paper for pattern

◆ 1¼ yd. (115 cm) of fusible interfacing

◆ Ten buttons

◆ 1¼ yd. (115 cm) of print fabric, for lining

Silks and velvets mix with delicate patterns in shades of purple.

1 From the prints and the silk and velvet, cut out twenty-
four 4-in. (10 cm) squares. From the silk cut out four
4 x 21½-in. (10 x 55-cm) strips. A rotary cutter, acrylic ruler,
and cutting mat are more accurate than scissors and will
allow you to cut two layers of silk at once. (The velvet should
be cut one layer at a time.)

2 To piece the front and back, join six assorted silk, velvet,
and print squares into a row, right sides together and raw
edges even, using ¼-in. (5-mm) seams. Make three more
rows in the same way, and then press all the seams open. For
the front, join one of these rows to a silk strip along the long
edges, right sides together and raw edges even, using ¼-in.
(5-mm) seams. Repeat for another silk strip and another row
of squares, then join the two sections in the same way, with
the silk strips and the rows of squares alternating. Press the
seams open. For the back, join the remaining two silk strips
and two rows of squares in the same way as for the front.

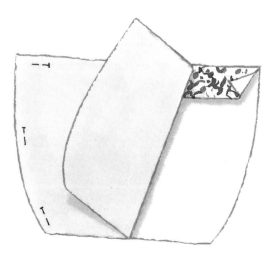

5 Turn the bag right side out. Sew five buttons onto the
upper silk strip at the front, and do the same for the
back, lining them up with the seams joining the squares.

6 At the top of the length of lining fabric, fold under
2½ in. (6 cm), and then pin the pattern to the lining
fabric so that the top edge of the pattern is on the fold. Cut
it out, then repeat to make a second lining piece. Unfold the
tops of the lining pieces and, right sides together, stitch
the two pieces together as in Step 4.

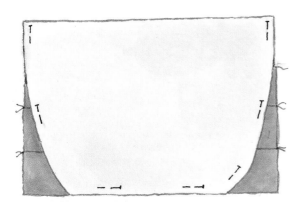

3 Enlarge and transfer the template from page 122 onto paper, and then cut out the pattern. Center and pin the pattern to the patchwork for the front and back pieces. Cut out both pieces.

4 Use the same pattern to cut out two pieces of fusible interfacing. Following the manufacturer's instructions, iron the interfacing to the wrong side of the patchwork front and back, making sure that the seam allowances are lying flat. Right sides together and raw edges even, pin and machine-stitch the front to the back around the sides and bottom using a ½-in. (1.5-cm) seam and pivoting at the bottom corners. Clip into the seam allowances on the curves, snip off the corners of the seam allowances at the bottom, and then press the seam open.

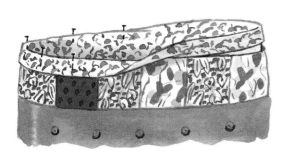

7 Turn under and press a double 1¼-in. (3-cm) hem at the top of the lining. Place the lining, wrong side out, inside the bag, pinning the hem in the lining over the top of the bag. Machine-stitch.

8 For the handles, cut two 3 x 23-in. (7.5 x 59-cm) strips of velvet. Fold one long edge of one strip into the center, wrong sides together, and hand-baste in place. Repeat for the other long edge of the strip. Turn in ¼ in. (5 mm) at each end, and then fold the strip in half lengthwise, enclosing all the raw edges. Pin and machine-stitch along the long edge and both ends. Make the second handle in the same way. Pin one end of each handle to the right side of the front and the other end of each handle to the right side of the back, positioning them evenly. Stitch as shown.

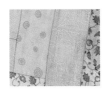

bamboo-handled tote bag

A pair of bamboo handles helps to transform scraps of assorted cotton prints into a pretty tote bag that is a handy enough size to be indispensable on any shopping trip. Inspired by log-cabin patchwork, this design is arranged in a more free and easy way than in the traditional log-cabin pattern. However, the overall effect is the same, with light and dark fabrics positioned diagonally opposite each other for a dramatic contrast.

The bag is 15¼ in. (38.5 cm) wide x 16 in. (42 cm) high (excluding handles).

You will need:

◆ ⅛ yd. (10 cm) each of cotton fabric in three light prints and three dark prints in shades of the same color, such as pink

◆ Rotary cutter, acrylic ruler, cutting mat (optional)

◆ Matching sewing thread

◆ ⅔ yd. (60 cm) of coordinating fabric, for lining

◆ ½ yd. (50 cm) of fusible interfacing

◆ Paper for pattern

◆ ½ yd. (50 cm) of faux suede in a coordinating color

◆ Pair of 6-in. (15-cm)-wide bamboo handles

◆ Fade-away marker pen

Light and dark shades of one color are often used in log-cabin designs.

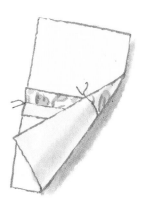

1 This design is made by joining strips to each other, starting with two center squares and working outward using progressively longer strips. Where possible, adjoining strips should be in different prints. From all six fabrics, cut long strips 1¾ in. (4.5 cm) wide, then cut them to the correct length as you need them. A rotary cutter, acrylic ruler, and cutting mat are more accurate than scissors and will allow you to cut two layers of fabric at a time. Start by cutting out a 1¾-in. (4.5-cm) square in each of two light fabrics, and pin them right sides together and raw edges even. Machine-stitch a ¼-in. (5-mm) seam. Press the seam open.

2 With the two joined squares arranged one above the other, join a dark strip to the left edge in the same way as in Step 1, trimming off the excess so both ends are even with the top and bottom edges of the two squares, and pressing the seam open. Join a light strip to the bottom of this strip and the adjoining square, again trimming the end so the raw edges are even, and again pressing the seam open.

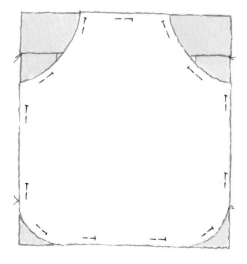

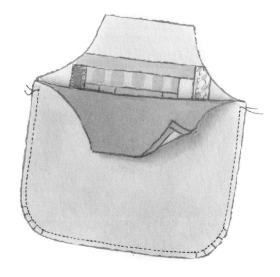

5 Enlarge and transfer the template from page 123 onto paper, then cut out the pattern. Pin the pattern to the patchwork and cut around it. Use the same pattern to cut out two pieces from the lining fabric and one from the faux suede.

6 Pin the patchwork to the faux suede, right sides together and raw edges even, and machine-stitch a ½-in. (1.5 cm) seam around the bottom and sides, starting and stopping ½ in. (1.5 cm) from where the bag begins to narrow. Do the same for the two lining pieces. Clip into the seam allowances on the curves at the bottom. Press open the seams. Press under a ½-in. (1.5-cm) hem along the raw edges of the bag and the lining. Clip into the seam allowances on the top curved edges (being careful not to clip too close to the folds).

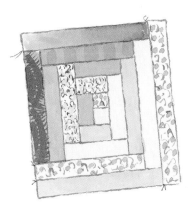

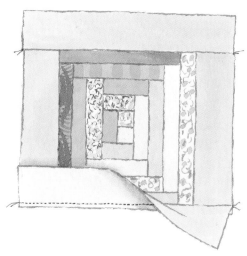

3 Using dark strips on the left side and the top, and light strips on the right side and the bottom, continue piecing in the same way. To create the pattern shown in the photograph, use the following sequence: top, right, top, left, bottom, right, left, top, left, bottom, right, top, bottom, right. Or, for a traditional log-cabin design, always work in the same direction and sequence—right, top, left, bottom, right, top, left, bottom, and so on (counterclockwise).

4 From the lining fabric, cut two strips 2¼-in. (5.5 cm) wide and as long as the length of the pieced section— about 13 in. (36 cm). Pin the long edge of one strip to one side edge, right sides together and raw edges even. Machine-stitch a ¼-in. (5-mm) seam, and press the seam open. Join the remaining strip to the other side edge. Now cut two strips 2¼ in. (5.5 cm) wide and as long as the width of the pieced section—about 16¼ in. (41.5 cm), and join these to the top and bottom edges in the same way, to complete the piecing of the front. Cut the interfacing to the same size as the front— about 16¼ x 17½ in. (41.5 x 45 cm) and, following the manufacturer's instructions, iron it to the wrong side, making sure that the seam allowances are flat.

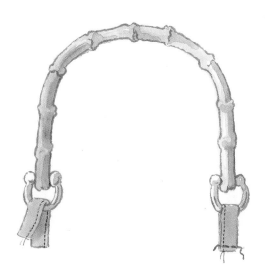

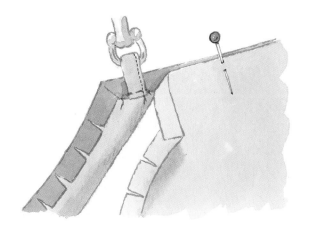

7 Using the bamboo handles as a guide, mark their positions with pins or a chalk pencil on the wrong side of the front and back at the top edges of the bag, an equal distance from each side seam. From one of the prints, cut a 1½ x 8-in. (4 x 21-cm) strip. Fold the long raw edges in to meet at the center, press, and then fold in half lengthwise, right side out, and press again. Topstitch close to the edge. Cut it into four equal lengths, and thread these carriers through the rings at the ends of the bamboo handles. Baste the ends of the carriers together. Pin and then baste them to the marked positions on the inside of the bag.

8 Turn the bag right side out. With the lining wrong side out, push it into the bag, matching the side seams. Carefully pin the lining to the bag around the top. Machine-stitch close to the edge, catching in the ends of the carriers at the same time and pivoting at the top corners. Remove the basting.

multicolored tote

*Even the slot-handles are part of the pattern of rectangular shapes in this sleek tote.
It is made from felted wool, preferably in at least four solid colors for maximum
impact. The back is the same as the front, and the two are joined by solid-color
sides and a base. Narrow braid, along with some stylized flowers made from the
same fabric as the rest of the bag and decorated with seed pearls, provides just enough extra
detail to contrast with the right angles of the pattern.*

The bag is 13½ in. (34.5 cm) wide x 17 in. (43 cm) high x 3¼ in. (8 cm) deep.

You will need:

- Paper for patterns
- Scraps of felted wool in at least four shades, such as pink, purple, yellow, and peach
- Rotary cutter, acrylic ruler, cutting mat (optional)
- Matching sewing thread
- Fade-away marker pen and fabric glue

- 6 x 14-in. (13 x 35-cm) piece of artist's plastic mesh (available from craft stores)
- 12 seed pearls
- 1 yd. (80 cm) of braid
- ⅔ yd. (50 cm) of fabric, for lining

Soft pastels and simple shapes are combined in this sturdy tote.

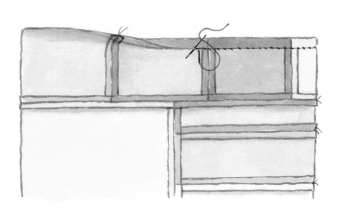

1 Enlarge and transfer the rectangular templates from page 124 onto paper, then cut out the patterns. From your chosen fabrics, cut out two pieces for each rectangular pattern (one of each pair will be used for the back of the bag and the other for the front), making sure that adjacent pieces will be in different colors and the tones will be balanced overall. Also cut out two 4¼ x 18-in. (11 x 46-cm) rectangles for the sides and one 4¼ x 14½-in. (11 x 37.5 cm) rectangle for the base, all from one color. A rotary cutter, acrylic ruler, and cutting mat are more accurate than scissors and will allow you to cut two layers of fabric at a time.

2 To piece the front, pin and machine-stitch the pieces, right sides together and raw edges even, using ¼-in. (5-mm) seams and pressing the seams open as you go, in the following sequence. Join the two pieces on the right of the center section, do the same for the four pieces on the left of the center section, and then join these two sections. Join the top four patches into a row, and the bottom two into another row, then join these rows to the top and bottom of the center section. Turn under and press ½ in. (1.5 cm) along the top edge; hand-sew in place. Make the back in the same way.

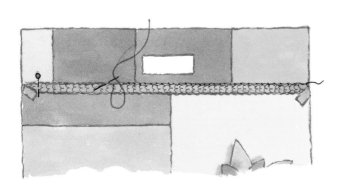

5 Cut a piece of braid the width of the front—about 14½ in. (37.5 cm)—and hand-sew it to the front along the seamline beneath the handle. Attach braid to the back in the same way. Turn under ½ in. (1.5 cm) on the top edge of each side piece; press and hand-sew in place.

6 Right sides together and raw edges even, pin the sides to the front along the side edges, and machine-stitch ½-in. (1.5-cm) seams, leaving the bottom ½ in. (1.5 cm) of the seams unstitched. Join the remaining side edges of the sides to the back in the same way. Right sides together and raw edges even, pin the base to the bag using ½-in. (1.5-cm) seams and allowing the unstitched portion of each side seam to open up at each corner, as shown. Adjust the size of the base or the width of the seams, if necessary, for a good fit. Machine-stitch, pivoting at the corners. Snip off the corners of the seam allowances, and press **the** seams open.

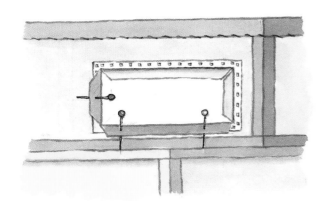

3 On the wrong side of the front, use a fade-away pen to draw a 2¾-in. (7-cm)-long line equal distances from the left and right sides and 1¼ in. (3 cm) from the folded top edge. Draw an identical line 1 in. (2.5 cm) beneath it, then draw lines joining the ends to form a rectangle; cut this out. From the plastic mesh, cut out a 2 x 3¾-in. (5 x 9.5-cm) rectangle, then cut a 1½ x 3¼-in. (4 x 8.5-cm) rectangular window in it, forming a frame. Place this over the rectangular slot cut in the front, on the wrong side. Clip diagonally into the corners of the fabric as far as the mesh, and fold each edge of the fabric back over the mesh. Pin and hand-sew in place. Make a slot in the back in the same way.

4 Transfer the two flower templates from page 124 onto paper. For the front of the bag, cut out two fabric flowers from each pattern, using a different color for each flower. Repeat to cut out four more flowers for the back. Seal the edges with fabric glue. When dry, sew the four smaller flowers on top of the four larger ones. Embellish each pair with three seed pearls, and hand-sew the flowers to the front and back.

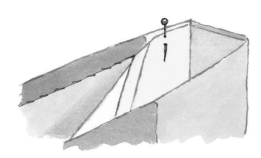

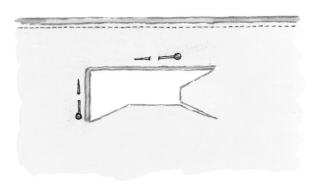

7 Cut a 3¼ x 13½-in. (8 x 34.5 cm) rectangle of plastic mesh (adjusting the size to fit the base if you adjusted that in Step 6). Hand-sew it to the wrong side of the base using a few stitches at each side. Turn the bag right side out. Using the templates, cut out a front, a back, two sides, and a base from the lining fabric. Join these pieces as in Step 6 to form the lining. Press under ⅝ in. (1.8 cm) at the top of the lining, and place the lining, wrong side out, inside the bag. The folded top edge of the lining should be ⅛ in. (3 mm) below the folded top edge of the bag. Pin and machine-stitch through all layers, about ⅛ in. (3 mm) below the folded top edge of the lining.

8 Use a fade-away pen to draw around the slot onto the lining of the front. Draw diagonal lines connecting the corners of the rectangle (forming an X-shape), and cut along these diagonal lines. Fold the resulting triangles to the wrong side of the lining, cut off the points, and slipstitch the lining to the wrong side of the bag around the opening. Repeat for the slot in the back.

diamond-patch tote

Although the front is made up entirely from diamond-shaped pieces of the same size and similar colors, this tote has a rich and sumptuous look. The small scale of the prints and the discreet sparkle of the sequins and tiny beads add just the right amount of delicate detail, while the back is a single piece of luxurious velvet. Be sure to include fabrics in light, medium, and dark tones to create the most pleasing effect.

The bag is 10 in. (25 cm) wide x 15½ in. (38 cm) high (excluding handles).

You will need:

- ◆ Paper for pattern
- ◆ Metal ruler and fade-away marker pen
- ◆ ⅛ yd. (10 cm) each of five print and two solid-color fabrics in coordinating colors, such as blues and greens
- ◆ Rotary cutter, acrylic ruler, cutting mat (optional)
- ◆ Matching sewing thread
- ◆ Set square (optional)

- ◆ ⅓ yd. (30 cm) each of fusible interfacing and lightweight polyester batting
- ◆ 26 sequins and 26 tiny beads, to match fabric
- ◆ ⅓ yd. (30 cm) of velvet in coordinating color
- ◆ ⅓ yd. (30 cm) of fabric in coordinating color, for lining
- ◆ Pair of 6-in. (15-cm)-wide black handles

Choose small prints in jewel shades for the diamond shapes making up this tote.

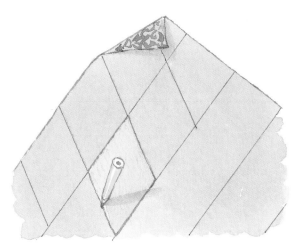

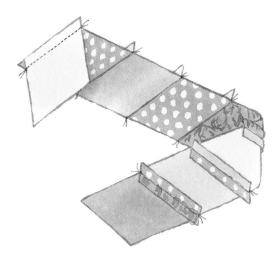

1 Transfer the template from page 125 onto paper, then cut out the pattern. Using a ruler and a fade-away pen or a pencil, mark 2¾-in. (7-cm) strips on one fabric; the total length of the strips will need to be about 33 in (84-cm). Place the pattern at one end of a strip, aligning two parallel edges of the pattern with those of the strip, and mark the other two sides of one diamond. Move the pattern along and mark more diamonds on the strips until you have nine or ten. Carefully cut out the diamonds. A rotary cutter, acrylic ruler, and cutting mat are more accurate than scissors and will allow you to cut two layers of fabric at a time. Repeat for the remaining fabrics, making 64 diamonds in all.

2 To piece the front, pin one diamond to a second one in a different fabric along one edge, right sides together and raw edges even, and machine-stitch a ¼-in. (5-mm) seam. Repeat to join more diamonds together so that you have a row of eight diamonds. Make seven more rows in the same way. Press open all the seams, and trim off the corners of the seam allowances even with the raw edges. Join the rows to each other in the same way, taking care to match the seamlines.

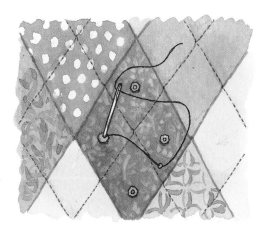

5 Hand-sew sequins with tiny beads in the centers to the diamonds in a symmetrical arrangement, knotting them individually. Cut out a piece of velvet and two pieces of lining, all the same size as the front.

6 Right sides together and raw edges even, pin the patchwork front to the velvet back around the sides and bottom. Machine-stitch a ½-in. (1.5-cm) seam, pivoting at the bottom corners. Press under a ½-in. (1.5-cm) seam at the top edges. Snip off the corners of the seam allowances at the bottom, and press open the seams. Trim away the batting within the seam allowance. Press. Make the lining in the same way.

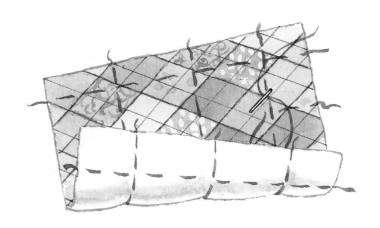

3 Turn the front as shown and use a ruler and a fade-away pen or a chalk pencil to draw a rectangle on it, with the points on the edges of the front. Use a set square or the corner of a piece of paper to make sure the corners of the rectangle are square. The rectangle will be about 11 x 16½ in. (28 x 41 cm). Carefully cut out the front along the drawn lines. Cut out a piece of interfacing and a piece of batting to the same size. Following the manufacturer's instructions, iron the interfacing to the wrong side of the patchwork, making sure that the seam allowances are flat.

4 On the right side of the front, use a fade-away pen and ruler to draw a grid of straight lines running through the center of each diamond, parallel to the sides of the diamonds. Pin the batting to the wrong side of the front, and hand-baste it in place using large running stitches from top to bottom, side to side, and corner to corner. Remove the pins. Now machine-stitch along the marked lines, starting from the center and working outward. Remove the basting.

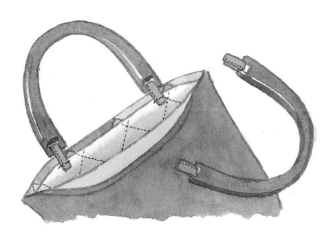

7 Using the black handles as a guide, mark their position with pins or the fade-away pen on the wrong side of the front and back at the top edges of the bag, equal distances from each side seam. From one of the prints, cut a 1½ x 8-in. (4 x 20-cm) strip. Fold the long raw edges in to meet at the center, press, and then fold in half lengthwise, right side out, and press again. Topstitch close to the edge. Cut it into four equal lengths, and thread these carriers through the holes at the ends of the black handles. Baste the ends of the carriers together. Pin and then baste them to the marked positions on the inside of the bag.

8 Turn the bag right side out. With the lining wrong side out, push it into the bag, matching the side seams. Carefully pin the top edge of the lining about ⅛ in. (3 mm) below the top of the bag. Machine-stitch close to the edge, catching in the ends of the carriers at the same time. Remove the basting.

girl's overnight tote

Any young girl will find this tote bag irresistible, whether for carrying pajamas to a sleepover or for storing treasures at home. Large plastic handles and a boxy shape make it very practical and roomy as well as versatile. The focus of the design, both front and back, is the fun novelty fabric used for six big patches, framed by solid-colored and striped fabric strips that are quick and easy to sew together.

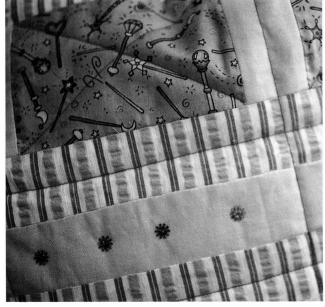

The bag is 15 in. (38 cm) wide x 16 in. (42 cm) high (excluding handles) x 2½ in. (6.5 cm) deep.

You will need:

◆ ½ yd. (50 cm) each of a novelty fabric, a solid-color fabric, and a striped fabric

◆ Rotary cutter, acrylic ruler, cutting mat (optional)

◆ Matching sewing thread

◆ 24 sequins

◆ ½ yd. (50 cm) of fusible interfacing

◆ ½ yd. (50 cm) of lightweight polyester batting

◆ Fade-away marker pen

◆ ⅔ yd. (60 cm) of muslin

◆ 3 x 15-in. (6.5 x 38-cm) piece of artist's plastic mesh (available from craft stores)

◆ Pair of 6-in. (15-cm)-wide clear plastic handles

Choose soft pastels or bright primary colors for this fun and modern tote.

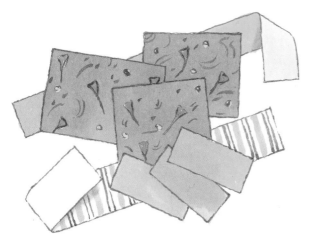

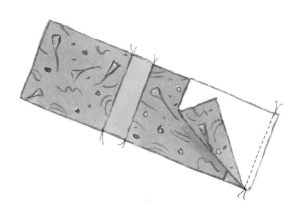

1 From the novelty fabric, cut out strips 3¾ in. (9.5 cm) wide, totaling at least 58 in. (1.5 m) in length. Cut the strips into eight rectangles 4½ in. (11.5 cm) long and four rectangles 5½ in. (14 cm) long. From the solid-color fabric, cut out a 1¾ x 30-in. (4.5 x 76-cm) strip; cut it into eight pieces 3¾ in. (9.5 cm) long. Also from this fabric, cut out two 2 x 16-in. (5 x 41-cm) strips and four 1¾ x 16-in. (4.5 x 41-cm) strips. From the striped fabric, cut out eight 2 x 16-in. (5 x 41-cm) strips. A rotary cutter, acrylic ruler, and cutting mat allow you to cut two layers at once.

2 Right sides together, raw edges even, and using ¼-in. (5-mm) seams, pin and machine-stitch the long edges of two short solid-color strips to the short edges of three novelty-fabric pieces. A narrower rectangle should be on each side and a wider one in the middle, separated by the solid-color strips. Press the seams open. Make three more pieced rows in the same way.

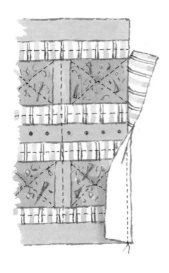

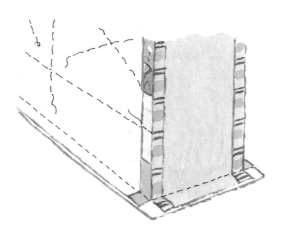

5 From the striped fabric, cut two 3½ x 14½-in. (9.5 x 38.5-cm) strips for the sides, and one 3½ x 16-in. (9.5 x 41-cm) strip for the base. Right sides together and raw edges even, pin the sides to the front along the side edges, with the top edge of each side extending ½ in. (1.5 cm) above the top seamline of the novelty-fabric pieces. Machine-stitch ½-in. (1.5-cm) seams, leaving the top and bottom ½ in. (1.5 cm) of the seams unstitched. Join the remaining side edges of the sides to the back in the same way. Press under ½ in. (1.5 cm) on the top edge of the front, sides, and back. Clip into the seam allowance of the bag side edge at the top of each side piece, and press under the seam allowance.

6 Right sides together and raw edges even, pin the base to the bag using ½-in. (1.5-cm) seams and allowing the unstitched portion of each side seam to open up at each corner, as shown. Adjust the size of the base or the width of the seams, if necessary, for a good fit. Machine-stitch, pivoting at the corners. Snip off the corners of the seam allowances, press the seams open, and trim away the batting within the seam allowance. Press under a ½-in. (1.5-cm) hem along the top raw edges. For the lining front and back, cut out two 16 x 17-in. (41 x 45-cm) rectangles from the muslin, along with the same strips as for the bag sides and base. (See Step 5.) Then make the lining as in Steps 5 and 6.

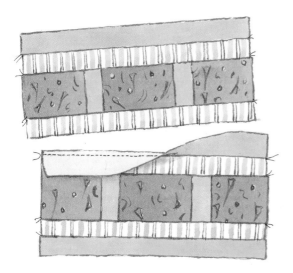

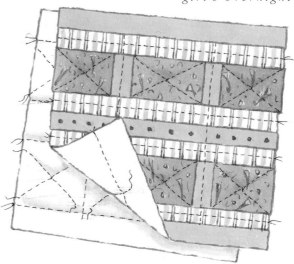

3 In the same way, join a striped strip to the top of each pieced row, and another to the bottom. Join a narrow solid-color strip to the top of one pieced section, and another to the bottom of another pieced section. Now join a wider solid-color strip to the other edge of each of these two pieced sections, so they are all joined, forming the front. Repeat with the remaining strips and pieced rows to make the back. Hand-sew sequins along the center of the middle strip on the front and back. Cut out two pieces each of interfacing and batting, to the size of the front and back—about 16 x 17 in. (41 x 45 cm). Following the manufacturer's instructions, iron the interfacing to the wrong side of the front and back, making sure that the seam allowances are flat.

4 On the right side of the front and back, use a fade-away pen and ruler to draw a straight line running through the center of each striped strip. Also draw vertical lines running through the center of each vertical solid-color strip, from the top striped strip to the bottom striped strip, and draw diagonal lines from corner to corner of each of the novelty-fabric rectangles. Pin the pieces of batting to the wrong side of the front and back, and hand-baste in place using large running stitches from top to bottom, side to side, and corner to corner. Remove the pins. Now machine-stitch along the marked lines, starting from the center and working outward. Remove the basting.

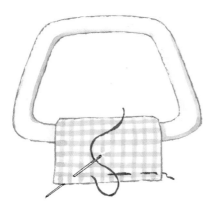

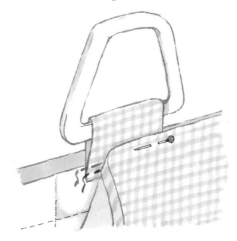

7 Cut a 2½ x 15-in. (6.5 x 38-cm) rectangle of plastic mesh (adjusting the size to fit the base if you adjusted that in Step 6). Hand-sew it to the wrong side of the base using a few stitches at each side. For the two carriers, cut two 3½ x 9-in. (9 x 23-cm) rectangles from the muslin. Fold one in half crosswise, right sides together. Machine-stitch a ¼-in. (5-mm) seam down the short edge. Press the seam open, turn right side out, and press again. Repeat for the other rectangle. Wrap each carrier around a handle, and baste the raw edges together at the end, then baste the ends of one carrier in the center of the top edge on the wrong side of the front, and the ends of the other in the same position on the wrong side of the back.

8 Turn the bag right side out and press. With the lining wrong side out, push it into the bag, matching the side seams. Carefully pin the lining to the bag around the top. Machine-stitch close to the edge, catching in the ends of the handles at the same time. Remove the basting.

gift bags

A handmade gift is always special, reflecting the time, effort, and skill you've put into making it. A patchwork bag will be particularly welcome because it is so useful. It is the perfect present, since you can personalize it according to the tastes, interests, and lifestyle of the recipient. By choosing the fabrics and trimmings carefully, you can even make it appropriate to the birthday, anniversary, holiday, or other occasion on which you are giving it. Any one of the bags included in this chapter would make a delightful gift, although once you have made it, you may decide that you simply cannot part with it.

wooden-handled bag

Taking its inspiration from a traditional knitting bag, this charming patchwork bag is a great way to make the most of pretty scraps that might have gone unused otherwise. A versatile size, it will make a popular gift. It could be used for a variety of purposes, such as a carryall for needlecraft materials or as a summer bag. At the top, where the patchwork wraps around the curved handles, the bag has a softly gathered look that contrasts well with the chunky wood. Bright rickrack and buttons add to the colorful effect.

The bag is 21 in. (54 cm) wide x 13 in. (34 cm) high (excluding handles).

You will need:

- ◆ Scraps of about five print fabrics
- ◆ Rotary cutter, acrylic ruler, cutting mat (optional)
- ◆ Matching sewing thread
- ◆ 1 yd. (1 m) of rickrack in first color, such as green

- ◆ 1⅔ yd. (1.6 m) of rickrack in second color, such as pink
- ◆ 25 assorted buttons
- ◆ Pair of 6-in. (15-cm)-wide round wooden handles

This bright carryall is a witty twist on Grandma's knitting bag.

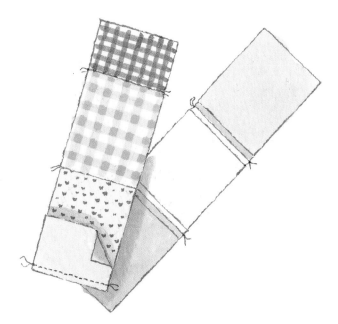

1 From the prints, cut out a total of thirty-six 4 x 5½-in. (10 x 14-cm) rectangles. A rotary cutter, acrylic ruler, and cutting mat are more accurate than scissors and will allow you to cut two layers of fabric at a time.

2 Join the short edges of two rectangles, right sides together and raw edges even, machine-stitching a ¼-in. (5-mm) seam. Join 11 more pairs in the same way. For six of these pairs, machine-stitch a single rectangle to one end. Cut the remaining six rectangles in half crosswise, forming 2¾ x 4-in. (4 x 7-cm) rectangles, and machine-stitch the long edges of these smaller rectangles to both ends of the six pairs of rectangles. Press all the seams open.

5 Cut two pieces of rickrack in the first color and four pieces in the second color, each to the same length as the height of the patchwork—about 15 in. (39 cm). Pin one piece in the first color down the center front seam of the patchwork and the other in this color down the center back seam. Pin two pieces in the second color down the seams nearest each side of the front, and the other two pieces down the corresponding seams on the back. Topstitch down the center of each piece of rickrack. Hand-sew buttons at the corners of some patches.

6 Starting 5½ in. (14 cm) from the top, machine-stitch for about 1½ in. (4 cm) along the side seamlines of the patchwork front and back to reinforce them. Right sides together and raw edges even, pin and machine-stitch the patchwork front to the patchwork back around the sides and bottom using a ¼-in. (5-mm) seam, starting and stopping 6¼ in. (16 cm) from the top, and pivoting at the bottom corners. Where the seam starts and finishes, clip into the seam allowances almost to the stitching. Snip off the corners of the seam allowances at the bottom, and press the seams open. Turn the bag right side out, and press.

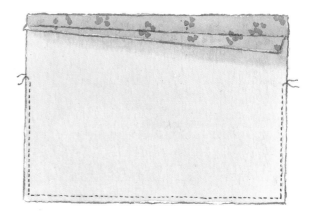

3 For the front, pin a three-patch row to a four-patch
row with right sides together and raw edges even, and
machine-stitch a ¼-in. (5-mm) seam. Add four more rows to
this section in the same way, alternating three-patch and
four-patch rows, to complete the front. Press the seams open
and trim the ends of the three-patch rows even with those of
the four-patch rows. Make the back in the same way, using
the remaining six rows.

4 From the lining fabric, cut out a front and a back the same
size as the patchwork front and back—about 15 x 21½ in.
(39 x 55 cm). Right sides together and raw edges even, pin the
lining front to the lining back at the sides. Using a ¼-in. (5-mm)
seam, stitch the sides and bottom: start and finish 6½ in. (16 cm)
from the top, pivoting at the bottom corners. Clip into the seam
allowances where the seams start and finish. Snip off the corners
of the seam allowances at the bottom. Press the seams open.

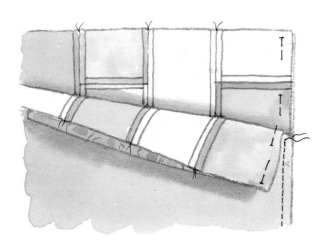

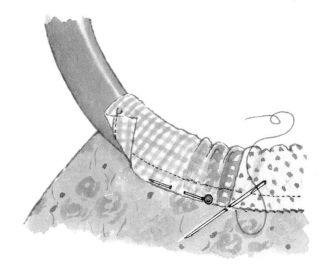

7 With the bag right side out and the lining wrong side
out, slip the bag inside the lining. With the top raw
edges even and the side seams matching, pin the raw side
edges of the lining front to those of the bag front, right sides
together; machine-stitch ¼-in. (5-mm) seams. Repeat to join
the lining back and the bag back at the sides. Press the seams
open. Now turn it right side out through one of the openings
between the lining and the bag at the top. Push the lining
inside the bag. Press.

8 On the front, press under ¼ in. (5 mm) at the top of the
lining and bag, treating the patchwork and lining as one
layer. Repeat for the back, then machine-stitch both hems.
Wrap the top of the front over one handle, with the lining on
the underside. Pin, and hand-sew the hemmed edge to the
inside of the bag. Repeat for the back and the other handle.

sailboat bag

Decorated with triangles resembling a flotilla of colorful sailboats, this charming bag will appeal to young and old alike. Its unusual handles are made from stiffened fabric, with a hand-sewn cutout in each. The bag in the photograph is made from just two fabrics—a solid color and a small print. The pattern of the fabric is varied so that the "sails" have some diversity while still looking like part of a set. You can use more than one print if you prefer, particularly if they coordinate in color or pattern.

The bag is 11¼ in. (29.5 cm) wide x 5½ in. (14.5 cm) high (excluding handles).

You will need:

- ⅔ yd. (50 cm) of one solid-color fabric
- ¼ yd. (20 cm), in total, of one or more print fabrics
- Rotary cutter, acrylic ruler, cutting mat (optional)
- Matching sewing thread
- Paper for patterns
- ½ yd. (40 cm) of fusible interfacing
- Fade-away marker pen
- Snap fastener (optional)

Repeated triangles give this bag a stylish graphic quality.

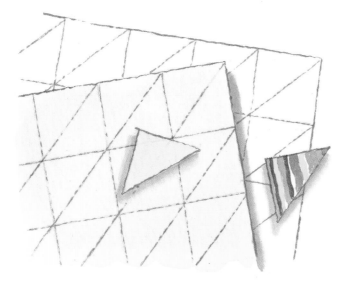

1 On the wrong side of the solid-color fabric, draw a grid of lines exactly 2¾ in. (6.6 cm) apart on the straight grain, until you have marked out eighteen 2¾-in. (6.6-cm) squares. Now draw straight lines, all in the same direction, between diagonally opposite corners of each square. Cut on the lines to make 36 triangles. Repeat to cut out 36 triangles from the print fabric. A rotary cutter, acrylic ruler, and cutting mat are more accurate than scissors and will allow you to cut two layers of fabric at a time.

2 Right sides together and raw edges even, pin a print triangle to a solid-color triangle along the long edges. Machine-stitch a ¼-in. (5-mm) seam. Repeat to join 35 more pairs of triangles. Press the seams open. Cut off the points of the seam allowances even with the raw edges. In the same way, join six of these pieced squares to form a row, with the print triangles all at the bottom. Repeat to make five more rows. Press the seams open. Right sides together and raw edges even, join three rows with ¼-in. (5-mm) seams along the long edges to form the front. Make the back from the remaining three rows in the same way. Press the seams open.

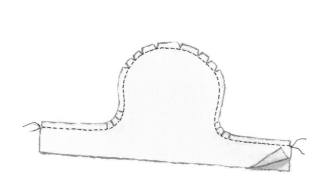
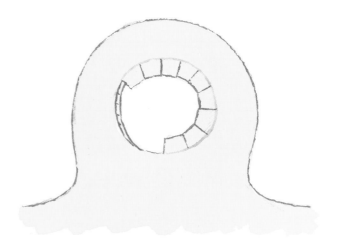

5 Pin one handle piece to a second around the top edge, right sides together and raw edges even. Stitch a ¼-in. (5-mm) seam, keeping the curve as smooth and even as possible. Clip into the seam allowances on the curves. Turn right side out and press. Using the fade-away pen, draw a smaller oval inside the existing oval, ¼ in. (5 mm) away from it.

6 Using very sharp scissors, carefully cut out the smaller oval from one layer and then from the other layer, making sure they match. On both layers, clip into the seam allowance all around the cutouts, almost as far as the outline of the larger oval. Turn in the seam allowances on both layers (tucking them between the two layers) along this outline, making the curve as smooth as you can; press. Repeat to make a second handle that matches the first.

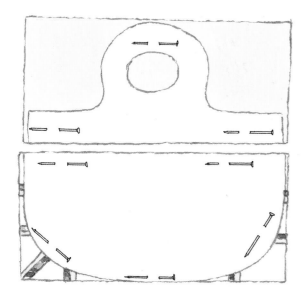

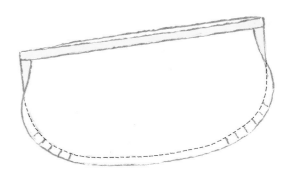

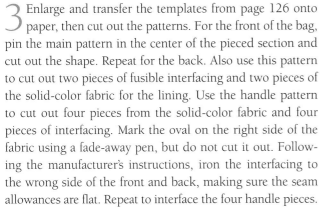

3 Enlarge and transfer the templates from page 126 onto paper, then cut out the patterns. For the front of the bag, pin the main pattern in the center of the pieced section and cut out the shape. Repeat for the back. Also use this pattern to cut out two pieces of fusible interfacing and two pieces of the solid-color fabric for the lining. Use the handle pattern to cut out four pieces from the solid-color fabric and four pieces of interfacing. Mark the oval on the right side of the fabric using a fade-away pen, but do not cut it out. Following the manufacturer's instructions, iron the interfacing to the wrong side of the front and back, making sure the seam allowances are flat. Repeat to interface the four handle pieces.

4 Right sides together and raw edges even, pin the front to the back around the sides and bottom. Machine-stitch a ¼-in. (5-mm) seam. Clip into the seam allowances on the curves. Press the seam open and press under a ¼-in. (5-mm) hem along the top raw edges. Make the lining from the two lining pieces in the same way. Turn the bag right side out and press.

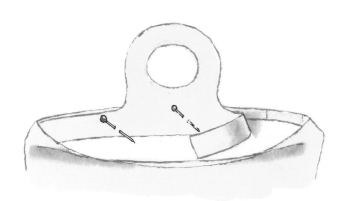

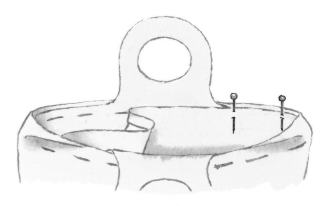

7 Pin and slipstitch the edges of the oval cutout on each handle together. Pin and hand-baste the bottom portion of one handle to the wrong side of the front at the top so that the top of the straight portion is just below the top edge. Pin and baste the other handle to the back in the same way and in exactly the same position.

8 With the lining wrong side out, push it into the bag, matching the side seams. Carefully pin the lining to the bag around the turned-under top edges. Machine-stitch close to the edge, catching in the straight portion of each handle at the same time. Remove the basting. If you wish, hand-sew the "ball" of a snap to the inside front at the center top, and the "socket" to the corresponding position on the inside back, sewing through the lining and handle only.

rose sparkle bag

A metallic piping inset into the side and bottom seams, combined with several shiny ribbon roses, adds just the right amount of bright detail to this pretty bag. The design of the front comprises a panel of triangles cut from a delicate floral print juxtaposed with a polka-dot fabric in the same colors, surrounded by strips of the same floral print. The handle is made from this print, too, while the back and lining are made from a large-scale print in the same colors.

 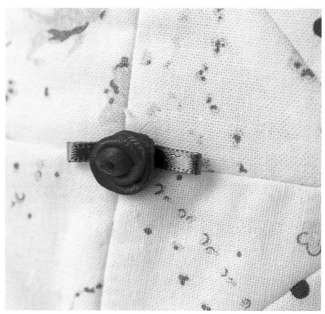

The bag is 12¾ in. (33.5 cm) wide x 7 in. (16.5 cm) high (excluding handle).

You will need:

◆ ¼ yd. (20 cm) of small-scale floral print fabric

◆ ⅛ yd. (10 cm) of a polka-dot fabric to match

◆ Rotary cutter, acrylic ruler, cutting mat (optional)

◆ Matching sewing thread

◆ ½ yd. (40 cm) of a coordinating large-scale floral print fabric

◆ ¼ yd. (20 cm) of fusible interfacing

◆ 1 yd. (80 cm) of ready-made narrow metallic piping

◆ Four small ribbon roses

◆ One snap fastener

A few ribbon roses and some piping add definition to the soft colors used for this bag.

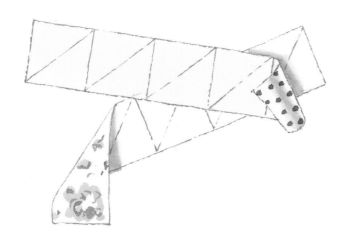

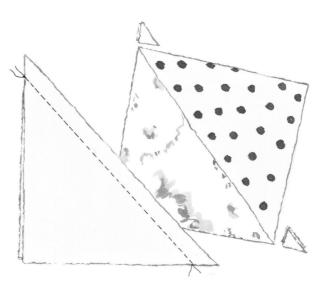

1 On the wrong side of the small-scale floral fabric, draw a grid of lines exactly 2¾ in. (7 cm) apart on the straight grain, until you have marked out five 2¾-in. (7-cm) squares. Now draw straight lines, all in the same direction, between diagonally opposite corners of each square. Cut on the lines, to make ten triangles. Repeat to cut out ten triangles from the polka-dot fabric. A rotary cutter, acrylic ruler, and cutting mat are more accurate than scissors and will allow you to cut two layers of fabric at a time.

2 Pin a floral triangle to a polka-dot triangle along the long edges, right sides together and raw edges even. Machine-stitch a ¼-in. (5-mm) seam. Repeat to join nine more pairs of triangles. Press the seams open. Cut off the points of the seam allowances even with the raw edges.

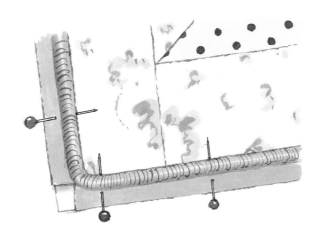

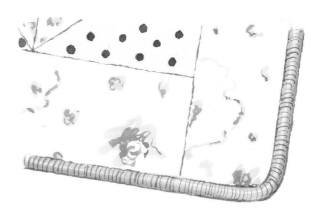

5 Cut out two pieces of interfacing and three pieces of large-scale floral fabric, each to the same size as the front—about 8 x 13¾ in. (19.5 x 36.5 cm). Following the manufacturer's instructions, iron the interfacing to the wrong side of the pieced front and one of the large-scale floral pieces, making sure the seam allowances are flat. Now pin the piping around the side and bottom edges of the front on the right side, with the piping ½ in. (1.5 cm) from the edge and facing inward. Clip into the piping seam allowance at the bottom corners. Cut off the excess piping after pinning it all around. With the piping foot or zipper foot on the machine (on the opposite side of the needle to the piping), machine-baste the piping to the fabric slightly less than ½ in. (1.5 cm) from the edge.

6 Right sides together and raw edges even, pin the back to the piped front around the sides and bottom. With the piping foot or zipper foot still on the machine, stitch a ½-in. (1.5-cm) seam, stitching very close to the piping. Snip off the corners of the seam allowances at the bottom, then press the seam open. Press under a ½-in. (1.5-cm) hem along the top raw edges. Make the lining from the two lining pieces in the same way, but without the piping. Turn the bag right side out, and press.

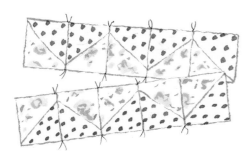

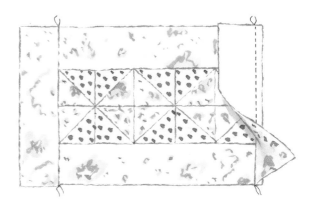

3 Right sides together, raw edges even, and machine-stitching ¼-in. (5-mm) seams, join five of these pieced squares together to form a row, turning some of the squares around so that they form the arrangement shown in the top row above. Repeat to make a second row that is the mirror image of the first, as shown in the bottom row above. Press the seams open.

4 Pin the lower edge of the first row to the top edge of the second row, right sides together and raw edges even. Machine-stitch a ¼-in. (5-mm) seam. Press the seam open. From the small-scale floral fabric, cut two strips, each 2¼ in. (5 cm) wide and as long as the width of the pieced section—about 10 in. (27.5 cm). Right sides together and raw edges even, pin them to the top and bottom of the pieced section. Stitch ¼-in. (5-cm) seams; press the seams open. Cut two more strips, each 2¼ in. (5 cm) wide and as long as the height of the pieced section—about 7¾ in. (19.5 cm). Join these strips to the sides of the pieced section in the same way, and press.

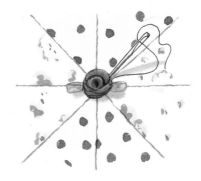

7 For the handle, cut a 3 x 10½-in. (7.5 x 27-cm) strip of the small-scale floral fabric. Fold it in half lengthwise, right sides together. Pin and machine-stitch a ¼-in. (5-mm) seam down the long edge. Now attach a safety pin to one end and thread it through the tube of fabric, pulling it through to turn the strap right side out. Press the handle flat. Pin and hand-baste one end of the handle to the bag front at the center of the top edge on the wrong side, and the other in the same position to the bag back.

8 Hand-sew four ribbon roses to the front of the bag. With the lining wrong side out, push it into the bag, matching the side seams. Carefully pin the lining to the bag around the turned-under top edges. Machine-stitch close to the edge, catching in the ends of the handle at the same time. Remove the basting. If you wish, hand-sew the "ball" of a snap to the inside front at the center top, and the "socket" to the corresponding position on the inside back, sewing through the lining and handle only.

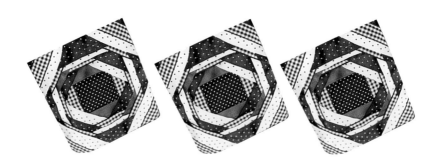

ribbon-motif flannel satchel

Both cozy and stylish, this handy-size satchel is made from soft but sturdy flannel. The unusual design of the wide handle allows you to sling the satchel over your arm with ease and comfort. The most delightful aspect, however, is the ribbon motif at the center of the front. Built up from pieces of ribbon that gradually increase in length, the motif is in sharp contrast to the soft flannel surround, which complements it beautifully. Choose dramatic black-and-white or colorful plaids to make the most of this striking effect.

The bag is 11½ in. (29 cm) wide x 11½ in. (29 cm) high (excluding 8-in. (20 cm) handle) x 2¼ in. (5.5 cm) deep.

You will need:

◆ 6-in. (15 cm) square of backing fabric, such as unbleached muslin

◆ ⅓ yd. (30 cm) of tiny polka-dot cotton fabric

◆ Assorted pin-dot, check, and solid-color ribbons, ½–1 in. (1–2.5 cm) wide

◆ ¾ yd. (70 cm) of flannel

◆ Matching sewing thread

◆ ½ yd. (40 cm) of polka-dot fabric, for lining

◆ Paper for pattern

◆ ⅓ yd. (30 cm) of sew-on hook-and-loop tape

Ribbons in crisp black-and-white patterns are set off by soft, dark flannel.

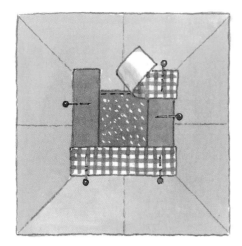

1 On a 6-in. (15-cm) square of backing fabric, mark the center point and the center of each side. Draw lines through the center to the center points on the sides and also out to the corners. These will serve as the placement lines for the ribbon motif. Cut a 1¾-in. (4.5-cm) square of tiny polka-dot fabric and hand-sew it in the center of the backing square around all four edges. Now make a frame for it by pinning lengths of one ribbon on either side and lengths of a second ribbon at the top and bottom, so that all the ribbons just cover the raw edges of the polka-dot square. Use the placement lines on the backing square as a guide to positioning. Hand-sew each one in place along the outside edge only.

2 Make another, larger frame in the same way, using four more pieces of ribbons. Set this frame as a diamond, "on point," adjusting the size so that, inside the frame, portions of the previous frame, but none of the backing fabric, are visible. Remember to sew only the outside edge. The third frame is made in the same way and is, again, a little larger, but positioned squarely, like the first. Continue making frames in this way, each slightly larger than the last, and with alternate frames on point. Finish with a frame on point, when almost none of the backing fabric is visible around the edge. Trim off excess ribbon ends, even with the edges of the backing square.

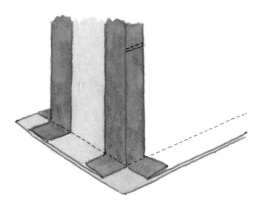

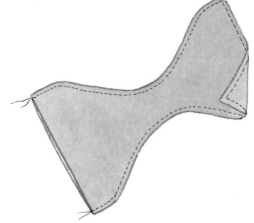

5 Right sides together and raw edges even, pin the sides to the front along the side edges, and machine-stitch ½-in. (1.5-cm) seams, leaving the bottom ½ in. (1.5 cm) of the seams unstitched. Join the remaining side edges of the sides to the back in the same way. Right sides together and raw edges even, pin the base to the bag using ½-in. (1.5-cm) seams and allowing the unstitched portion of each side seam to open up at each corner, as shown. Adjust the size of the base or the width of the seams, if necessary, for a good fit. Machine-stitch, pivoting at the corners. Snip off the corners of the seam allowances, and press the seams open. Press under ½ in. (1.5 cm) along the top edge of the bag. Make the lining in the same way. Turn the bag right side out; press.

6 For the handle, enlarge and transfer the template from page 127 onto paper, adjusting the enlargement so that the ends are ½ in. (1 cm) wider than the front of the bag; cut out the pattern. From the flannel and the tiny polka-dot fabric, cut out one piece each. Right sides together and raw edges even, pin the polka-dot piece to the flannel around both sides and the deeper (back) end, leaving the shallower (front) end open. Machine-stitch a ¼-in. (5mm) seam, pivoting at the corners. Snip off the corners of the seam allowances at the stitched end, and clip into the seam allowances on the curves. Press the seam open, turn right side out, and press.

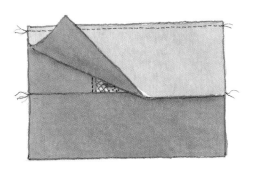

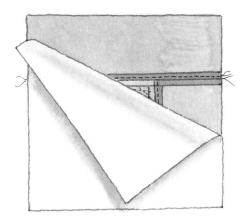

3 From the flannel, cut two 4½-in. (11-cm) squares. Press under ¼ in. (5 mm) on one edge of each. With the folds next to the motif, pin them to the left and right sides of the motif, 4 in. (10 cm) apart, centered between the top and bottom edges—overlap the ribbons so that none of the backing square is visible. Topstitch close to both folded edges. Cut two 4½ x 12½-in. (11 x 32-cm) flannel rectangles. With right sides together and the raw edges even with the ends of the other flannel pieces, pin them above and below the ribbon motif, overlapping the ribbons so that no backing fabric shows. Machine-stitch ¼-in. (5-mm) seams. Press the seams open, and topstitch close to the edge of each seam.

4 From the flannel, cut out a piece for the back to the same size as the pieced front—about 12½ in. (32-cm) square, one strip for the base 3¼ in. (8.5 cm) wide and as long as the width of the front, and two strips for the sides 3¼ in. (8.5 cm) wide and as long as the height of the front. From the lining fabric, cut out two pieces the size of the front, and three strips the same size as the flannel strips for the lining base and sides. From the interfacing, cut out two pieces the size of the front, and three strips the same size as the flannel strips. Following the manufacturer's instructions, iron the interfacing to the wrong side of the front, back, base, and sides, making sure the seam allowances are lying flat.

7 Pin and machine-stitch the "loop" strip of a length of hook-and-loop tape to the polka-dot side of the handle at the stitched end, close to the edge. On the right side of the bag back, pin and machine-stitch the "hook" strip of the tape 1 in. (2.5 cm) from the top edge. Machine-baste a ¼-in. (5-mm) seam at the unstitched end.

8 Pin and hand-baste the basted end of the handle to the wrong side of the bag front at the top. With the lining wrong side out, push it into the bag, matching the side seams. Carefully pin the lining to the bag around the turned-under top edges. Machine-stitch close to the edge, catching in the bottom portion of the handle at the same time. Remove the hand-basting. Fasten the free end of the handle to the back of the bag using the hook-and-loop tape.

quilted circle bag

Delicate antique silk can sometimes be found at antique fairs in the form of petticoats or other garments. Although some areas may be too worn, you may be able to salvage enough to make a beautiful evening bag. For this small, circular bag, one piece of vintage silk has been dyed, pieced, and quilted by hand, and then decorated with minuscule beads and sequins. With the soft sheen of the silk and the delicate texture of the quilting, this is a bag that is elegant enough for any occasion.

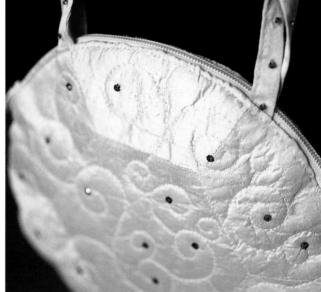

The bag is 6¾ in. (16 cm) in diameter (excluding handles).

You will need:

◆ 12-in. (30-cm) square of antique silk

◆ Mild laundry detergent

◆ Cold-water hand dye with fixative and non-iodized salt (optional)

◆ Cardstock for patterns and stiff paper for backing papers

◆ Matching sewing thread and quilting thread

◆ Fade-away marker pen

◆ One 8-in. (20-cm) square each of fusible interfacing and lightweight polyester batting

◆ 8-in. (20-cm) square of velvet in color to harmonize with silk

◆ ¼ yd. (20-cm) of raw silk, for lining

◆ Small quilting hoop

◆ 20 small sequins and 34 small seed beads

◆ 8-in. (20-cm) matching zipper

A delicate peach-color silk is complemented by intricate quilting.

1 Trim the silk into one piece and hand-wash it in mild detergent, then rinse it well. If you wish to hand-dye the silk, mix the dye following the manufacturer's instructions, and do a small test patch. Once you are happy with the result, immerse the fabric into the dye bath and, wearing rubber gloves, agitate it gently but constantly for about five minutes. Check the color by rinsing the fabric under cold water; if it is too pale, agitate it in the dye bath for five more minutes. Rinse well in cold water until the water runs clear, pat with a dish towel to remove most of the moisture, and then press with a cool iron while still damp.

2 Transfer the two templates from page 125 onto cardstock, then cut out the patterns. Draw around the patterns onto stiff paper, and cut out so that you have one hexagon and six of the wedge-shapes to use as backing papers. Place the backing papers on the wrong side of the silk, aligning the inner straight edge (the one opposite the curved edge) with the grain of the silk. With a pencil or fade-away pen, draw the outline of each, following the shape of the backing paper but adding a ¼-in. (5-mm) seam allowance all around. Carefully cut out the silk patches.

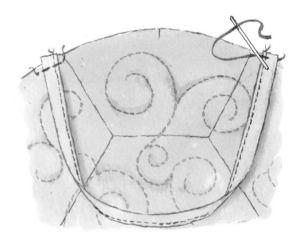

5 Cut one piece each of interfacing, batting, and velvet, and two pieces of raw silk, all to the same size as the pieced front. Following the manufacturer's instructions, iron the interfacing to the wrong side of the front, making sure that the seam allowances are flat. Use a fade-away pen to draw a curly design on the right side of the silk front. Pin the batting to the interfaced side of the front. Hand-baste it in place using large running stitches from top to bottom, side to side, and diagonally. Remove the pins, place the front in the hoop, and, with quilting thread, hand-quilt along the marked lines using backstitch. Remove the basting. Hand-sew the sequins to the front, then remove the fabric from the hoop.

6 For the handles, cut two 1½ x 11¾-in. (4 x 30-cm) strips from the antique silk. Fold the long raw edges in to meet at the center, press, and then fold in half lengthwise, right side out, and press again. Topstitch close to the edge. With the fade-away pen, mark the center-top point of the front, then mark points 1¾ in. (4.5 cm) either side of it. Right sides together and raw edges even, baste the ends of one handle to the top at these points. Baste the other handle to the velvet back in the same way. Place the zipper in the center at the top of the front, mark the ends on the wrong side using the fade-away pen, and then put the zipper aside.

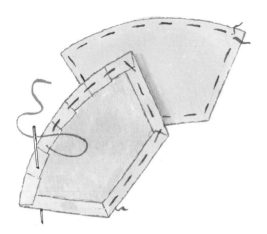

3 With the backing paper in the center of the wrong side of a silk patch, fold one seam allowance over the paper, so the edge of the paper is even with the fold. Hand-baste through the fabric and paper. Trim the corner of the seam allowance even with the raw edge. Fold over the next seam allowance in the same way, and baste across the corner and down the center of the seam allowance. Repeat for the remaining sides (clipping into the seam allowance before basting on the curve). Baste each piece to a backing paper in the same way.

4 Right sides together and corners matching, place one wedge-shape on top of the hexagon so that one edge of the hexagon is even with the other piece's inner straight edge. Hand-sew the two edges together from corner to corner using small stitches, without catching the backing paper in the stitches. Backstitch at each corner to secure. In the same way, sew the other wedge-shapes to the hexagon and then sew the adjacent edges of the wedge-shapes together, to complete the piecing of the front. Remove the basting threads and the backing papers. Press.

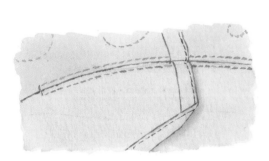

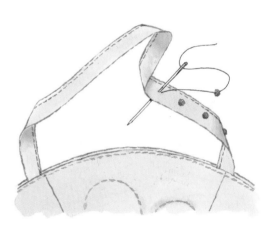

7 Pin the front to the back at the top edge, right sides together and raw edges even. Machine-stitch a ½-in. (1.5-cm) seam for about 1 in. (2.5 cm) beyond each marked point, and machine-baste a ½-in. (1.5-cm) seam between those points. Press the seam open, then open out the fabric, wrong side up. Pin the closed zipper, face down, between the marked points, with the teeth along the seamline. Avoid pinning through the handles on the other side. Hand-baste the zipper in place, avoiding the handles. Remove the pins and turn the bag over. Using the zipper foot and keeping the handles out of the way, topstitch down each side of the zipper and across the ends just beyond the top and bottom stops. Remove the hand- and machine-basting, and open the zipper.

8 Right sides together and raw edges even, pin the front to the back, and machine-stitch a ½-in. (1.5-cm) seam all the way around (as a continuation of the seams either end of the zipper). Clip into the seam allowances on the curve, and trim away the batting within the seam allowance. Press the seam open, and turn the bag right side out. Make the lining in the same way but with no zipper—instead, leave an opening ¼ in. (5 mm) longer than the zipper opening and press under the seam allowances on the opening. With the lining wrong side out, push it into the bag, matching the seams. Hand-sew the turned-under edges to the inside of the zipper opening using backstitch. Finally, hand-sew about 17 beads to each handle, spacing them evenly.

folded-star clutch bag

Make the most of the vivid colors available in silk with this elegant clutch. The simple shape is remarkably versatile and provides an excellent background for the beautiful folded-star patchwork medallion in contrasting hues. Made by layering rectangles that have been folded into triangles and hand-sewn in place, the medallion is small and the patchwork is not too time-consuming. Its impact, however, is enormous, providing the finishing touch to a truly beautiful gift.

The bag is 8 in. (20.5 cm) wide x 5 in. (13 cm) high.

You will need:

◆ Paper for patterns

◆ 16 x 20-in. (40.5 x 51-cm) piece of silk in a jewel color, such as jade green

◆ 10 x 16-in. (25.5 x 40.5-cm) piece of lightweight polyester batting

◆ Matching sewing thread

◆ Scrap of backing fabric, such as unbleached muslin

◆ Scraps of silk in two other, contrasting jewel colors, such as red and blue

◆ Compass and fabric marker pen

◆ 4-in. (10-cm) square of fusible interfacing

Rich red, blue, and green silks are combined in this beautiful clutch bag.

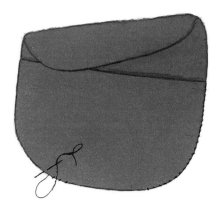

1 To make the pattern for the bag, draw an 8½ x 14-in. (21.5 x 35.5-cm) rectangle on the paper, and cut it out. Fold up one short edge by 5¼ in. (13.5 cm). At one corner of the folded end, mark points 3 in. (7.5 cm) each side of the corner. Do the same at the unfolded end of the rectangle. Draw a smooth curve between the two points at each of these two corners, and cut out the shape. Unfold the paper, and fold it in half lengthwise. Draw around the curves, cut them out, and unfold the pattern. Use the pattern to cut two pieces of silk in the first color (green) and one piece of batting.

2 Place one silk piece on top of the other, with right sides together, and lay the batting on top. Pin and machine-stitch a ¼-in. (5-mm) seam all around the edge, leaving an opening. Trim away the batting within the seam allowance. Press the seam open and turn the silk right side out. Press, turn in the seam allowances on the opening, and slipstitch. Now fold up the smaller portion of the bag, pin the edges together, and slipstitch. Fold the remaining portion down over this, forming the flap.

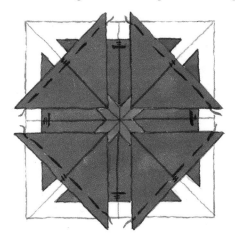

5 Make up eight triangles in the second color (red), as in Step 3. Pin four of them on top of the green ones, in the same positions but with the points ¼ in. (1 cm) from the center. Pin four more red triangles in between and overlapping the first four red ones, lining up the points with the first four red points, and with the centers even with the diagonal placement lines. Stab-stitch the points. Hand-baste the outer edges in place through all layers, and remove the pins.

6 Make up eight triangles in the third color (blue), as in Step 3, and arrange them on top of the red ones in the same position but with the points ½ in. (2 cm) from the center. For the first four blue triangles, the centers should be even with the diagonal placement lines; for the four on top, the centers should be even with the vertical/horizontal lines. Stab-stitch the points in place through all layers. The motif should be marginally more than 3½ in. (9 cm) across. Now use a compass to make paper patterns for circles that have diameters of 3½ in. (9 cm), 3 in. (7.5 cm), and 2½ in. (6.5 cm). Center the largest circle over the front of the folded-star motif, and pin the circle to the motif. Cut around it, trimming off the outer points of the last round of triangles. Also cut out a piece of interfacing using this large circle pattern.

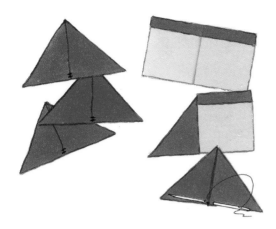

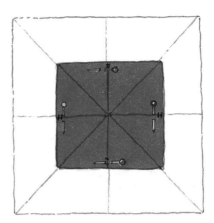

3 For the patchwork, cut four 1½ x 2½-in. (4 x 6.5-cm) silk rectangles from the first color (green). Place one of the rectangles wrong side up, fold down ¼ in. (5 mm) along one long edge, and press. Fold the rectangle in half crosswise to find the center, press to mark the center, and then open it up again. Now fold the two top corners (on the folded edge) down to the center of the unfolded edge, and press. Hand-sew the folded edges together, and make two backstitches through all thicknesses, ⅛ in. (3 mm) from the base of the triangle. Repeat to make triangles from the other three rectangles.

4 On a 4-in. (10-cm) square of backing fabric, mark the center point and the center of each side. With a pencil, draw lines through the center to the center points on the sides and also out to the corners, to serve as placement lines. Pin the four green triangles on the backing square, with the folded edges on top, the centers even with the vertical and horizontal placement lines, and the points just meeting at the center. Stab-stitch the points in place (inserting the needle vertically). Hand-baste the outer edges to the backing square, and remove the pins.

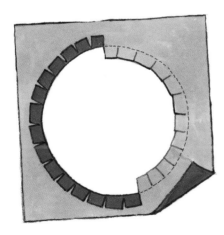

7 For the red frame encircling the motif, cut out a 5-in. (13-cm) square from the red silk. Now use a fabric marker and the other two patterns to draw two circles in the center of the red square on the wrong side. Machine-stitch around the larger circle, and then cut out the smaller circle. Clip into the seam allowance of this "window" almost up to the stitching, and turn the seam allowance to the wrong side along the stitching. Press, pin, and hand-baste in place.

8 Center the silk frame over the folded-star motif and slipstitch the inner edge to the motif. Trim the square into a circle that is ½ in. (1.5 cm) larger all around than the outer edge of the medallion. Fold the fabric to the back around the outer edge, and hand-sew it in place on the back. Following the manufacturer's instructions, iron the circle of interfacing to the back of the medallion. Hand-sew the medallion to the bag flap.

cosmetic bag

Perfect as either an elegant cosmetic holder or an evening clutch, this bag is quickly made using just two different silk fabrics. The alternating bands of color on the front and back create a bold striped effect, which is subtly complemented by diagonal machine-quilting that matches one of the fabrics. A zipper provides a neat closure at the top, while sequins and a tassel add a touch of glitz.

The bag is 11¾ in. (29.5 cm) wide x 5 in. (12 cm) high.

You will need:

◆ ¼ yd. (20 cm) each of raw silk in two contrasting colors, such as turquoise and gold

◆ Rotary cutter, acrylic ruler, cutting mat (optional)

◆ Matching sewing thread

◆ One 13-in. (33-cm) square each of fusible interfacing and lightweight polyester batting

◆ Paper for pattern

◆ Fade-away pen

◆ Thread in deeper shade of main color, for quilting

◆ 12 sequins, 12 tiny beads, and one tassel

◆ 9-in. (23-cm) matching zipper

◆ ¼ yd. (20 cm) of floral fabric, for lining

A gold tassel and sequins are the finishing touch to this striped silk bag.

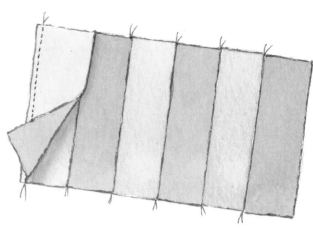

1 From the raw silk, cut out eight strips of the first color and six of the second, each measuring 2¼ x 6 in. (5.5 x 15 cm). A rotary cutter, acrylic ruler, and cutting mat are more accurate than scissors and will allow you to cut two layers of fabric at a time.

2 Right sides together and raw edges even, pin one long edge of a strip of the first color to a strip of the second color. Machine-stitch a ¼-in. (5-mm) seam. Join five more strips to these two in the same way, alternating colors, to form a rectangle with seven stripes; this will be the front. Make the back in the same way, using the remaining strips. Press open all the seams.

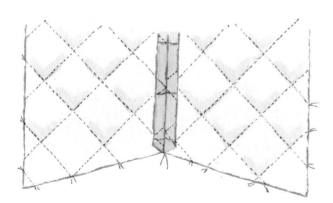

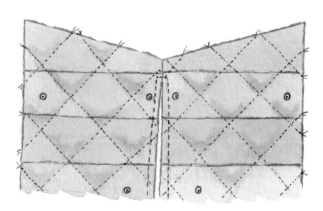

5 Right sides together and raw edges even, pin the front to the back along the top edge, matching the stripes. Machine-baste a ½-in. (1.5-cm) seam along this edge. Press the seam open, then open the fabric out, wrong side up.

6 Pin the closed zipper to the seam allowance, face down, centering it between the ends of the seam and with the teeth along the seamline. Hand-baste the zipper in place. Remove the pins and turn the bag over. With the zipper foot on the machine (on the opposite side of the needle to the zipper), topstitch down each side of the zipper and across the ends just beyond the top and bottom stops. Remove the hand- and machine-basting, and open the zipper.

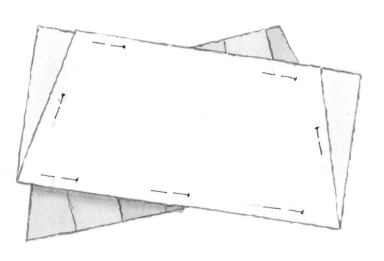

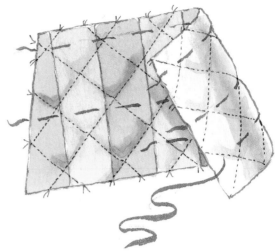

3 Cut two pieces of interfacing to the same size as the front and back—about 6 x 12¾ in. (15 x 32.5 cm). Following the manufacturer's instructions, iron them to the wrong side of the front and back, making sure that the seam allowances are flat. Enlarge and transfer the template from page 126 onto paper, then cut out the pattern. Pin the pattern to the patchwork front and cut around it; repeat for the patchwork back, making sure that the stripes are positioned exactly the same. Also use the pattern to cut out two pieces of lining and two of batting.

4 With a fade-away pen, draw a grid of diagonal lines 1½ in. (4 cm) apart on the right side of the patchwork front and back. Pin the batting to the wrong side of the front and back. Using a contrasting thread, hand-baste the layers together from top to bottom, side to side, and diagonally. Remove the pins, and with the deeper shade of thread, machine-quilt along the marked lines. Take out the basting. Hand-sew about six sequins with beads in the centers to the front; repeat for the back.

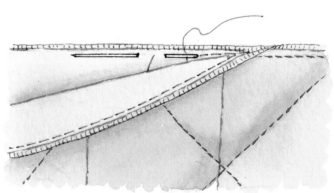

7 Right sides together and raw edges even, pin the front to the back around the remaining edges. Machine-stitch a ½-in. (1.5-cm) seam from one end of the zipper around to the other end of the zipper, pivoting the stitching at the corners. Snip off the corners of the seam allowances and trim away the batting within the seam allowances. Press the seam open, then turn the bag right side out.

8 Make the lining in the same way but with no zipper— instead, leave an opening ¼ in. (5 mm) longer than the zipper opening and press under the seam allowances on the opening. With the lining wrong side out, push it into the bag, matching the seams. Hand-sew the turned-under edges to the inside of the zipper opening using backstitch. Hand-sew the tassel to the zipper with matching thread.

evening bags

Perhaps the most inspiring and enjoyable bags to make, evening bags allow you to indulge yourself with glamour and glitz to your heart's content. Because the bags are relatively small, they require only tiny amounts of fabric and trimmings, so you can use expensive materials, such as vintage silk and beautiful beads. Their small scale also means you can use elaborate techniques like hand-quilting or cathedral-window patchwork, without the project becoming too time-consuming. Accordingly, this chapter presents dazzling designs made with irresistible materials, from organdy and jewel-colored silk to sparkly sequins.

star-patch silk shoulder bag

Chinese-style silk fabrics stitched into a patchwork star design make a stunning shoulder bag for evening. Choose colors to coordinate with your favorite party outfit, or stick to pinks and similar soft tones for a delicate look that enhances the intricate design and exquisite fabric. A bold, shimmering bead trim on the bottom edge finishes the bag beautifully. For extra sparkle, you could sew tiny glass beads onto the star, either randomly or at the corner points.

The bag is 8 in. (20 cm) wide x 9 in. (22.5 cm) high (excluding handle and bead trim).

You will need:

◆ Paper for patterns

◆ Scraps of three patterned silk fabrics

◆ ½ yd. (40 cm) of a fourth patterned silk fabric

◆ Rotary cutter, acrylic ruler, cutting mat (optional)

◆ Matching sewing thread

◆ ⅓ yd. (30 cm) of beaded trim

The sheen of silk in soft colors highlights the patchwork of this shoulder bag.

1 Transfer the templates from page 127 onto paper, then cut out the patterns. From the first and second fabrics, cut out three diamonds each; from the third fabric, 12 small triangles; and from the fourth fabric, four large triangles. A rotary cutter, acrylic ruler, and cutting mat are more accurate than scissors and will allow you to cut two layers of fabric at a time.

2 Right sides together and raw edges even, pin the longest edge of a small triangle to one edge of a diamond. Machine-stitch a ¼-in. (5-mm) seam. In the same way, join a second small triangle to the adjacent side of the diamond (the other side of the smaller angle). Repeat to join the ten remaining small triangles to the five remaining diamonds. Press the seams open.

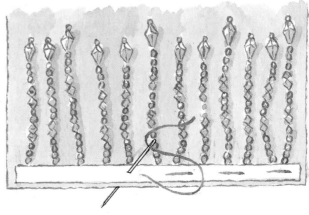

5 From the fourth fabric, cut out four 2¼-in. (6-cm) squares, two strips 2¼ in. (6 cm) wide and as long as the height of the pieced section—about 7½ in. (19 cm), and two strips 2¼ in. (6 cm) wide and as long as the width of the pieced section—about 6½ in. (16.5 cm). Right sides together and raw edges even, pin the longer strips to the sides of the pieced section, and stitch a ¼-in. (5-mm) seam. Press the seams open. In the same way, join a square to each end of the two shorter strips, press the seams open, and then join these two sections to the top and bottom of the pieced section, matching the seams. Press the seams open. This completes the piecing of the front.

6 From the fourth fabric, cut three pieces the same size as the front—about 9 in. (23 cm) wide x 10 in. (25.5 cm) high—for the back and lining, and one 1¾ x 36-in. (4.5 x 91-cm) strip for the strap. Hand-baste the beaded trim to the lower edge of the back piece on the right side, with the tape portion within the ½-in. (1.5-cm) seam allowance; avoid having beads within ½ in. (1.5 cm) of each end, but the tape should extend to less than ½ in. (1.5 cm) from each end. Right sides together and raw edges even, pin the front to the back around the sides and bottom. Machine-stitch a ½-in. (1.5 cm) seam: pivot at the bottom corners and avoid the beads. Snip off the corners of the seam allowances at the bottom. Press the seam open. Turn right side out. Press.

3 With right sides together, raw edges even, and seams matching, pin one diamond/triangle to another. Machine-stitch a ¼-in. (5-mm) seam. Join another diamond/triangle to this section in the same way, and continue until all the diamond/triangles are joined. Press the seams open.

4 Now pin the long edge of one large triangle to the outside edges of the two triangles at one corner of the star panel, right sides together and raw edges even; machine-stitch a ¼-in. (5-mm) seam. Repeat to join the other three large triangles to the other three corners.

7 For the strap, fold the long strip in half lengthwise, right sides together. Pin and machine-stitch a ¼-in. (5-mm) seam down the long edge. Attach a safety pin to one end, thread the safety pin through the tube of fabric, and pull it through to turn the strap right side out. Press the strap flat. With raw edges even, pin the ends to the side seams at the top of the bag on the right side.

8 Right sides together and raw edges even, pin one lining piece to the other along the sides. Machine-stitch ½-in. (1.5-cm) seams, and press the seams open. With the bag right side out and the lining wrong side out, slip the lining over the bag. With the top raw edges even and the side seams matching, pin the top edge of the lining to the top edge of the bag, and machine-stitch a ½-in. (1.5-cm) seam all around the top. Now pull the lining away from the bag, so it is right side out. Press the seams, and press under ½-in. (1.5-cm) seam allowances on the bottom edge of the lining. Slipstitch these edges together and push the lining inside the bag; press.

leaf-print evening bag

In this exquisite evening bag, square and rectangular patches in two colors of silk are arranged to frame a pair of delicate hand-printed leaf motifs. Tiny glass beads form an inner frame for each leaf print, while a matching braid decorated with sparkly glass beading finishes off the top edge of the bag. The velvet back and the cord also match, to avoid any jarring contrasts.

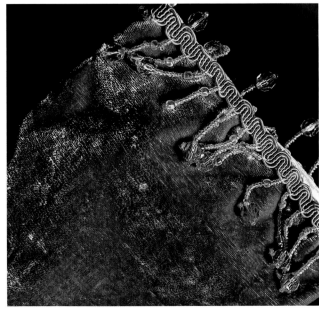

The bag is 7 in. (17.5 cm) wide x 10⅛ in. (25.5 cm) high.

You will need:

◆ ⅓ yd. (30 cm) of raw silk in a pale color, such as gold

◆ ⅛ yd. (10 cm) of raw silk in a contrasting color, such as eau de nil

◆ Rotary cutter, acrylic ruler, cutting mat (optional)

◆ Artist's paintbrush and black fabric paint

◆ Ivy leaf from the garden

◆ Matching sewing thread

◆ 9 x 12-in. (23 x 30-cm) piece of fusible interfacing

◆ Fade-away marker pen and small quilting hoop

◆ About 84 tiny glass beads

◆ 9 x 12-in. (23 x 30-cm) piece of velvet, to match one silk color

◆ 1 yd. (80 cm) of ¼-in. (5-mm)-wide matching cord

◆ ½ yd. (40 cm) of glass-beaded ⅜-in. (1-cm)-wide braid

◆ One snap fastener

The motifs were hand-printed using an ivy leaf and fabric paint.

1 From the pale color, cut out two 2¾-in. (7-cm) squares, two 4-in. (10-cm) squares, and two 2¾ x 3-in. (7 x 7.5-cm) rectangles. From the contrasting color, cut out one 2¾ x 3½-in. (7 x 8.5-cm) rectangle, one 3 x 3½-in. (7.5 x 8.5cm) rectangle, and two 2¾ x 6½-in. (7 x 16-cm) rectangles. A rotary cutter, acrylic ruler, and cutting mat are more accurate than scissors and will allow you to cut two layers of fabric at a time.

2 Practice the following technique on scraps of silk, and once you are satisfied with it, make leaf prints in the centers of the two larger pale silk squares. With the brush, paint a small amount of black fabric paint onto the leaf. Place the leaf on the fabric and press down firmly, without allowing it to slide, and then gently lift it away. When the prints are dry, place a clean cloth over them and, following the manufacturer's instructions, iron them to fix the image. Trim to 3½ in. (8.5 cm) square, with the motif centered.

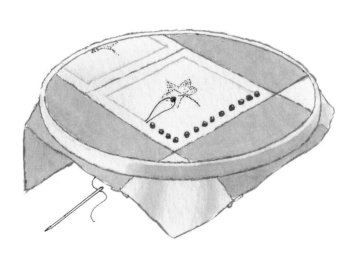

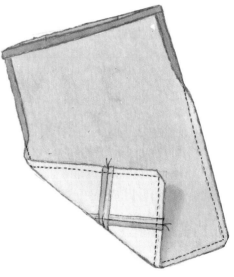

5 Cut the interfacing to the same size as the front. Following the manufacturer's instructions, iron it to the wrong side of the patchwork, making sure that the seam allowances are flat. Using a fade-away pen, mark a square "frame" around each leaf motif ⅜ in. (1 cm) inside the edge. Place the patchwork in a hoop and hand-sew beads around the marked lines.

6 From the velvet, cut out a back piece the same size as the front. From the pale silk, cut out two pieces the same size as the front, for the lining. Pin the patchwork to the velvet, right sides together and raw edges even. Machine-stitch a ½-in. (1.5-cm) seam around the sides and bottom, pivoting at the corners. Snip off the corners of the seam allowances at the bottom. Press open the seams. Make the lining in the same way. Press under a ½-in. (1.5-cm) hem along the top edges of the bag, and a ½-in. (1.5-cm) hem along the top edges of the lining.

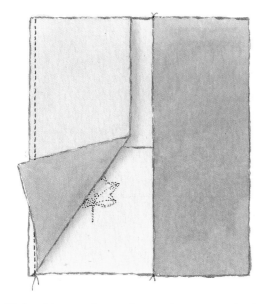

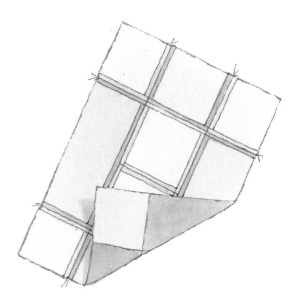

3 Right sides together and raw edges even, pin the lower edge of one printed square to the top edge of the other. Machine-stitch a ¼-in. (5-mm) seam. Press the seam open. In the same way, join the long edges of the longest contrasting rectangles to the side edges of the leaf-printed squares.

4 In the same way, join one long edge of a pale rectangle to the short edge of the larger remaining contrasting rectangle. Now join the other pale rectangle to the other short edge of the contrasting rectangle, remembering to press the seams open as you go. Stitch this row to the top of the pieced section, matching seamlines carefully. Repeat to stitch the two small pale squares on either side of the small contrasting rectangle, and stitch this to the bottom of the pieced section to complete the piecing of the front.

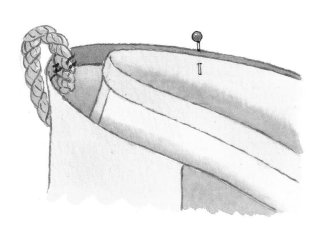

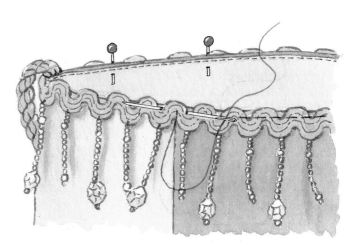

7 Cut a 30-in. (76-cm) length of cord and hand-sew the ends inside the top of the bag, at the sides. Turn the bag right side out. With the lining wrong side out, push it inside the bag, matching the seams. Pin and then machine-stitch the top edge of the lining just below the top of the bag.

8 Using a backstitch, pin and then hand-sew the beaded braid around the top of the bag. Hand-sew a snap at the center of the top of the bag on the inside, with the "socket" portion on the front and the "ball" portion on the back.

 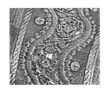  

glitzy evening bag

In this unusual evening bag, the combination of velvet, shot silk, and organza creates a sumptuous look that is perfect for special occasions. The miniature duffle-bag design, in which tubular sides are sewn onto a square base and lined with silk, is ideal for holding brushes, eye pencils, mascara, and other party essentials. A silver cord provides an elegant yet practical drawstring at the top, while silver braid in two widths and some sparkling sequins add more than a hint of glitz.

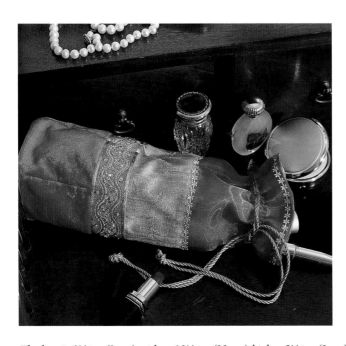 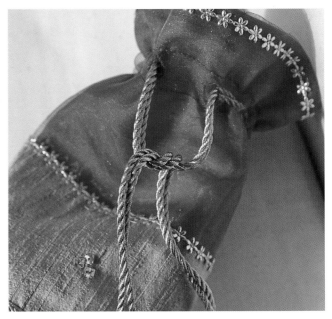

The bag is 3½ in. (9 cm) wide x 12½ in. (32 cm) high x 3½ in. (9 cm) deep.

You will need:

- ⅛ yd. (10 cm) of shot silk in a color such as pinkish orange
- ¼ yd. (20 cm) of velvet in a color such as pinkish red
- ¼ yd. (20 cm) of organza in a color, such as pink
- Matching sewing thread
- ¼ yd. (20 cm) of beaded silver-and-pink braid, about 1½ in. (4 cm) wide
- Silver thread
- ⅓ yd. (30 cm) of narrow silver daisy braid

- 12 silver sequins
- ½ yd. (40 cm) of silk in a fourth color, such as peach, for lining
- 3½ in. (9-cm) square of artist's plastic mesh (available from craft stores)
- Fade-away marker pen and safety pin
- 1½ yd. (1.4 m) of narrow silver cord

Bright-colored shot silk, velvet, and organza dazzle with silver.

1 From the shot silk, cut four rectangles, each measuring 4 x 5 in. (10 x 13 cm). From the velvet, cut four 4-in. (10-cm) squares. From the organza, cut one 5 x 14½-in. (3 x 37-cm) rectangle.

2 Right sides together, join the shot silk pieces in a row, machine-stitching the long edges together using ¼-in. (5-mm) seams. Do the same for the velvet squares, but leave the bottom ½ in. (1.5 cm) of each seam unstitched. Press the seams open. Pin the two rows with right sides together and raw edges even, carefully matching the seams, and stitch a ¼-in (5-mm) seam. Join the long edge of the organza rectangle to the shot silk in the same way. Press the seams open.

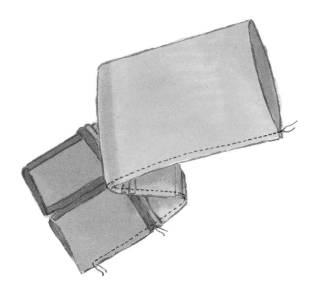

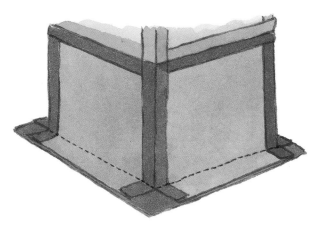

5 With right sides together, raw edges even, and the lining extended as shown, pin the long edges of the whole piece together. Machine-stitch a ¼-in. (5-mm) seam to create a long tube, leaving the bottom ½ in. (1.5 cm) of the seam unstitched.

6 For the base, cut a 4½-in. (12-cm) square of the velvet. Right sides together and raw edges even, pin the base to the lower edge of the bag using ½-in. (1.5-cm) seams and allowing the unstitched portion of each seam of the patchwork to open up at each corner of the base, as shown. Adjust the size of the base or the width of the seams if necessary. Machine-stitch, pivoting at the corners. Snip off the corners of the seam allowances, and press the seams open. Cut out a 3½-in. (9-cm) square of plastic mesh (adjusting the size to fit the base if necessary). Hand-sew it to the wrong side of the base using a few stitches at each side. Turn the bag right side out; press.

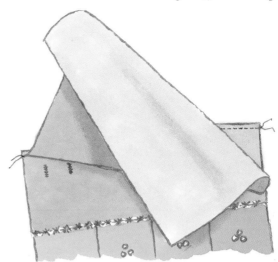

3 Pin the wider braid to the right side of the shot silk, with the lower edge of the braid even with the seamline joining the shot silk to the velvet. Hand-sew the braid in place using small, neat running stitches and matching silver thread. Pin and hand-sew the daisy braid along the seamline joining the shot silk to the organza, again with small running stitches and silver thread. Hand-sew four groups of three silver sequins to the shot silk, spacing them evenly.

4 Mark a point 1½ in. (4 cm) from the top left corner of the organza. Following the machine instructions, make a buttonhole ¾ in. (2 cm) long at right angles to the top edge, with the top at the marked point. Make a second buttonhole of the same size parallel to the first and the same distance from the top, 1¼ in. (4 cm) to the right of the first. Cut a 13 x 14½ in. (34 x 37-cm) piece of lining silk. Pin the longer edge to the top of the organza, right sides together and raw edges even, then machine-stitch a ¼-in (5-mm) seam. Press the seam open.

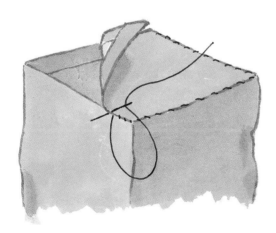

7 Press under ½ in (1.5 cm). on the remaining raw edge of the lining. Using a fade-away pen, mark points in line with the four corners of the bag base (one of the points will be at the seam). Cut out a 4½-in. (12-cm) square of the lining silk, and press under ½ in. (1.5 cm) on each edge. With the lining right side out and the marked points on the lining aligned with the corners of the square, slipstitch the square to the lining. Push the lining into the bag, and press.

8 Using the fade-away pen, mark a line around the bag 1¼ in. (3 cm) down from the top edge, and a second line ¾ in. (2 cm) farther down—these should run through the top and bottom of the buttonholes made in Step 4. Machine-stitch along these lines, through both the lining and the organza, forming a casing. Double the cord and thread it onto a safety pin. Insert the safety pin and doubled cord through one buttonhole, and push it through the casing, pulling it out through the other buttonhole. Remove the safety pin and knot the ends. Finally, pin and hand-sew the daisy braid near the top using small running stitches and silver thread.

harlequin drawstring bag

Hand-sewn hexagons encircle this irresistible drawstring bag in a harlequin-style decoration. Fabricated in luminous silks, it looks wonderful as an evening bag, yet it is surprisingly easy to make. The design simply comprises two contrasting silk circles that are sewn together, with a cord drawstring that slots through a casing. The hexagon decoration that is sewn onto the outside of the bag introduces a third silk, in a soft plaid incorporating tones of the other two.

The bag is 9 in. (20 cm) wide x 6 in. (15 cm) high x 9 in. (20 cm) deep.

You will need:

- ◆ Paper and cardstock for patterns
- ◆ 15-in. (38-cm) length of string
- ◆ 1 yd. (1 m) of fusible interfacing
- ◆ ⅔ yd. (60 cm) each of silk in first color, such as blue, and second color, such as pink

- ◆ Fade-away marker pen
- ◆ Scrap of plaid silk fabric
- ◆ Matching sewing thread
- ◆ 4½ yd. (4.1 m) of narrow cord

With its irresistible colors and sheen, silk is ideal for an evening bag.

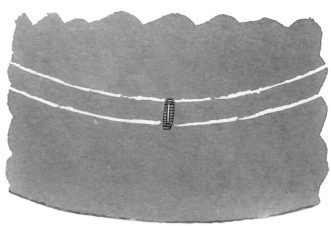

1 To make a circular paper pattern, cut out a 22-in. (56-cm) square of paper and fold it into fourths. Tie one end of the string to a pencil, and hold the other end at the folded corner of the square (the center when it is unfolded) so that you can use them like a compass. Adjust the string until the pencil reaches to the edge of the paper with the string taut, then draw a quarter-circle. Cut this out and unfold it—the pattern should be a circle with a 22-in. (56-cm) diameter.

2 Use the pattern to cut out one circle each of interfacing and silk in the first color (blue) and second color (pink). Following the manufacturer's instructions, iron the interfacing to the wrong side of the blue silk circle. Using a fadeaway pen, mark a circle on the right side of the blue silk 2½ in. (6.5 cm) from the edge, and another circle ¾ in. (2 cm) inside it. These will be the casing stitching lines. Following your machine manufacturer's instructions, make a buttonhole between the marked casing lines and at right angles to them, and make a second one on the opposite side of the circle. (Alternatively, cut a slit and then work buttonhole stitch around it.)

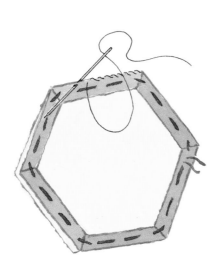

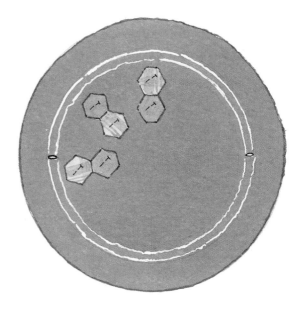

5 Right sides together and corners matching, hand-sew a pink patch to a plaid patch from corner to corner using small, neat stitches. Backstitch at each corner to secure. Join the remaining patches in the same way so that you have a total of eight pairs of patches.

6 Arrange the patches evenly around the blue circle on the right side, so that the outer edge of each is ½ in. (1 cm) inside the inner casing line, with the plaid patch on the outside for every other pair. Pin and hand-sew in place. Remove the basting.

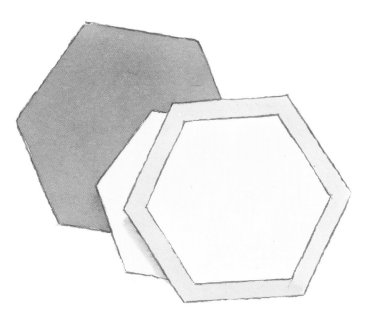

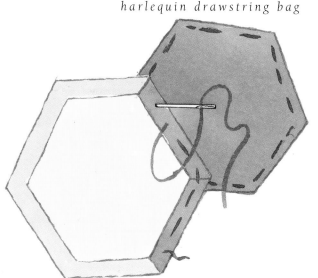

3 Transfer both hexagon templates from page 125 onto cardstock, then cut out the two patterns. Use the smaller pattern to cut out 16 hexagons from the interfacing. Use the larger pattern to cut out eight hexagons from the second color of silk (pink) and eight from the plaid silk. Following the manufacturer's instructions, iron the interfacing to the center of each silk hexagon on the wrong side.

4 On each hexagon, fold one seam allowance over the interfacing, so the edge of the interfacing is even with the fold. Hand-baste through the silk and interfacing. Trim the corner of the seam allowance even with the raw edge. Fold over the next seam allowance in the same way, and baste across the corner and down the center of the seam allowance. Repeat for the remaining sides. Press.

7 Right sides together and raw edges even, pin the pink circle to the blue one around the edges. Machine-stitch a ¼-in. (5-mm) seam, leaving an opening. Turn right side out. Press the seam. Press under the seam allowance on the opening edges, and slipstitch the opening closed. Machine-stitch around the two casing lines.

8 Cut the cord in half, attach a safety pin to one end, and thread it through one buttonhole, around the casing and out of the same buttonhole. Remove the safety pin, and hand-sew the ends of the cord together. Work the cord through the casing so that the joined ends do not show and the visible cord is seamless. Repeat for the second length of cord, threading it into and out of the other buttonhole.

  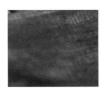 

plaid taffeta shoulder bag

Prepare to dazzle with this bright silk and plaid taffeta evening shoulder bag. The front and back of the bag are made using the cathedral-window patchwork technique, in which squares are folded and refolded, and then the edges are rolled over the other squares and hand-stitched in place. Incorporating jewel-colored silks, the patchwork is reminiscent of the stained glass of cathedral windows. Once completed, the patchwork front and back are hand-sewn together, lined, and finished with a cord, sequins, and beads.

The bag is 7 in. (18 cm) square.

You will need:

◆ ½ yd. (40 cm) of plaid taffeta

◆ Rotary cutter, acrylic ruler, cutting mat (optional)

◆ Matching sewing thread

◆ Scraps of silk in two solid colors, such as blue and green

◆ 8 x 20-in. (20 x 50-cm) piece of silk in a third solid color, such as red

◆ 8 small beads and 3 large star sequins

◆ 1½ yd. (1.4 m) of cord

Made from richly colored taffeta and silk, this bag is small but packs a punch.

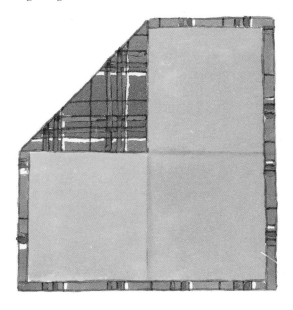

1 From the plaid taffeta, cut out eight 7½-in. (19-cm) squares on the straight of grain. From the three silks, cut a total of eight 2½-in. (6.5-cm) squares. A rotary cutter, acrylic ruler, and cutting mat are more accurate than scissors and will allow you to cut two layers of fabric at a time. On the first plaid square, with the wrong side up, press ¼ in. (5 mm) to the wrong side on all four edges. Fold the square in half both ways to find the center point; press; and then open it out again. Fold in each corner of the square to meet at the center point. Press.

2 Fold in each corner of the folded square to the center, forming a 3½-in. (9-cm) square. Press and pin. Stab-stitch (inserting the needle vertically) the four center points in place. Repeat with the remaining plaid squares.

5 Repeat Steps 3 and 4 for two more plaid squares and another silk square. Pin the first pair of plaid taffeta squares to the second pair along one long edge, folded sides together and edges even. Hand-sew them together along the pinned edge; open out; and press. Pin two more silk squares on point over the seam joining adjacent plaid squares so that the four silk squares form one big diamond shape. Finish the edges as in Step 4. This forms the front. Repeat Steps 3, 4, and 5 to make the back.

6 Hand-sew a bead at the center of each of the four plaid squares on the front, and a cluster of three star sequins at the center point. Do the same on the back. Pin the front to the back, wrong sides together and edges even. Hand-sew the side and bottom edges together using tiny, neat stitches.

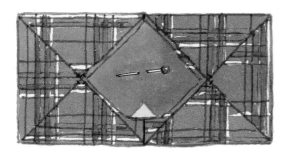

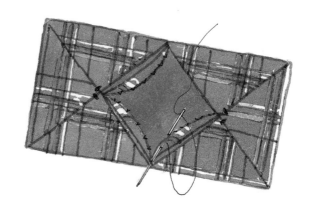

3 Place two plaid squares with the folded sides together and the edges even. Hand-sew them together along one edge, and then open out the squares and press. Pin one of the silk squares as a diamond, "on point," over the seam joining the two plaid taffeta squares, as shown.

4 Roll back the folded edge of one plaid square over the raw edge of the silk square that is on top of it. Arrange the rolled-back edge to form a smooth curve, tapering to a point at each end. Slipstitch it invisibly in place, sewing through all of the layers and making a double backstitch at each end. Do the same for the other three edges.

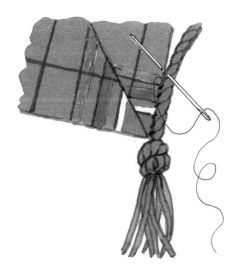

7 For the lining front and back, cut two 7½-in. (19 cm) squares of silk in the third color. Right sides together and raw edges even, pin one to the other along the side and bottom edges. Machine-stitch a ¼-in. (5-mm) seam, pivoting at the bottom corners. Snip off the corners of the seam allowances at the bottom. Press the seam open, and press under ¼ in. (5 mm) all around the top edge. With the lining wrong side out, slide it inside the bag and slipstitch it in place around the top edge.

8 Knot both ends of the cord about 1½ in. (4 cm) from the end. Unravel the cord beneath the knots to create tassels. Hand-sew the cord to the side edges, with the knots at the bottom corners, and the excess cord at the top of the bag to serve as a strap.

techniques

Patchwork and quilting are versatile crafts that are suited to bags of all types, from clutches to totes. They incorporate designs that are as simple or complex as you would like them to be. Learning the simple techniques explained here will enable you to make the projects in the book and also to design your own bags as well.

Basic equipment

Apart from a sewing machine, little equipment is required. In addition to the items listed under "You will need" for each project, you should have the following on hand:
◆ pins (long, fine ones are best)
◆ scissors (large shears for cutting out fabric, small pointy scissors for clipping seam allowances and cutting threads, and separate scissors for cutting out paper patterns)
◆ a pencil (either regular or dressmaker's colored pencils)
◆ a straightedge such as a ruler or yardstick
◆ an iron

Special equipment

Items that are optional or needed occasionally are listed under "You will need" for the relevant projects. These include:
◆ a fade-away marker pen (markings disappear after about 24 hours)
◆ a set square, which is handy for drawing square corners
◆ an embroidery or quilting hoop, consisting of two rings that fit together tightly and hold the fabric taut between them
◆ a cutting mat (for use with a rotary cutter) made from a self-healing material and marked with a cutting grid
◆ a rotary cutter, which allows you to cut through two to four layers at once with great accuracy
◆ a 6 x 24-in. (15 x 60-cm) acrylic ruler

To use a rotary cutter, place the fabric on the mat, and lay the ruler over the layers of fabric so that its right edge is along

the marked cutting line on the fabric. Remove the guard from the rotary cutter. With your left hand pressing hard on

the ruler and fabric, well away from the edge, and your right hand holding the rotary cutter flat against the ruler and at a 45-degree angle to the mat, push the cutter down and away from you. (If you are left-handed, reverse these instructions.) When you are finished cutting, put the guard back on the rotary cutter immediately.

IMPORTANT: When cutting out, use either non-metric measurements or metric measurements (shown in parentheses). Never mix the two systems interchangeably, because the equivalents are only approximate.

Obtaining fabrics

The beauty of patchwork is that you can use up leftover scraps or inexpensive remnants from fabric shops. Old clothes can be recycled, too, so long as the pieces you use are not too worn. Avoid combining old with new, because the stronger fabric will cause the weaker one to wear faster.

Buying new fabric is another option, since only small amounts are needed. Fabric sold by the yard/metre is usually at least 42 in./107 cm wide, so fabric widths are not given in the "You will need" lists for each project. If less than ⅛ yd. (10 cm) is required, scraps or small pieces are specified.

Some fabric shops, quilt shops, and mail-order suppliers sell packs or bundles of coordinated "fat quarters"—half a yard cut in half crosswise, to produce 18 x 22-in. (45 x 56-cm) pieces— or small squares of fabric. The amounts are economical and convenient, and the prints and colors often work together better than ones you might put together individually.

Fabric guidelines

When different fabrics are used for one bag, they should ideally be of equal weight and thickness. The best fabrics are firmly woven and not prone to stretching or fraying.
◆ Cotton is the most suitable. For a sturdy tote bag, canvas, denim, cotton duck, or corduroy work well.
◆ Wool that isn't coarsely woven can also be used. Felted wool (wool that has been treated to reduce and mat the fibers) is particularly attractive for a bag, because it is soft and dense and does not fray. Man-made or synthetic fibers, such as polyester, are not easy to use because they are crease-resistant and therefore are difficult to fold.

◆ Silk can look wonderful, though it is not as easy to work with and not as durable as cotton. Cover the work table with an old sheet to prevent the silk from slipping when you are cutting it. Use only very fine pins and place them only within the seam allowances. If two layers slip when you are stitching them together, place tissue paper between the layers, then remove it afterward. Press silk using the lowest setting on the iron.

◆ Velvet looks sumptuous but needs special care in preparation. When cutting it out, make sure that all the pieces run in the same direction. Velvet that has been cut so that the pile feels smooth when stroked from bottom to top will look richer. Cut out one layer at a time. Hand-basting the seams before stitching will help prevent the fabric from slipping, as will placing tissue paper between the layers and then removing it after stitching. A machine attachment called a walking foot (or an even-feed foot) will also help prevent the fabric from slipping. Always iron velvet on the wrong side, with a towel on the ironing board.

Interfacing and batting

Most bags, except those intended to look soft and floppy, are interfaced to give them structure. Fusible nonwoven interfacing is the easiest type to use. If you want to prevent the bag from sagging, choose a heavyweight fusible interfacing.

Cut the interfacing to the size of the front and back. Lay it with the adhesive side down on the wrong side of the fabric, making sure the patchwork seam allowances are all flat. Steam-press it in place, using a damp press cloth on top to protect the iron and create extra steam. Follow the manufacturer's instructions carefully, because each product is slightly different.

Another, firmer type of interfacing is lightweight artist's plastic mesh, available from craft stores. It is useful for stiffening the base of a bag that is not flat, or the area around a cut-out handle slot, as on page 53.

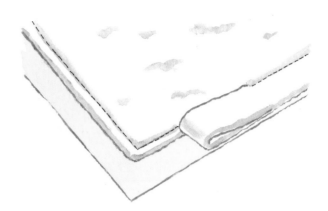

Some of the projects in this book are backed with batting and then quilted. Polyester batting is preferable to cotton, because cotton batting has to be closely quilted to prevent lumps and it is not washable. Cut batting to the same size as the front and back. Then, once the seams are stitched, trim away the batting that is within the seam allowances so that the seams will lie flat.

Handles and trimmings

Some of the projects feature handles made from fabric or cord. Other projects use store-bought handles. Available from craft stores or fabric shops, they come in a number of colors and materials. They are attached with carriers, small pieces of fabric, or ribbon that loop over the handles and are sewn to the top of the bag. (See page 119 for instructions on how to make and attach carriers and fabric handles.)

Trimmings provide the finishing touch to many a stylish bag, so take inspiration from the wide range of buttons, sequins, beads, seed pearls, ribbons, rickracks, braids, fringes, and tassels that are available today. They are so stunning that you could design an entire bag around a single trimming. Where possible, sew the trimmings to the front or back prior to lining the bag.

Combining prints

Choose fabrics that have something in common, such as color, but also contrast in some way. Look for:
◆ Contrasts in scale—although bags are small, you can use dramatic large-scale prints for the back or lining, or for pieces you carefully position when cutting them out.
◆ Contrasts in density—between widely spaced motifs and compact designs.
◆ Contrasts between random overall designs and those with repeated motifs.
◆ Contrasts between checks or stripes and florals. Stripes add vitality and provide visual relief from busy prints.

Planning the design

Once you have chosen your fabrics, plan the arrangement before cutting out the pieces or sewing them together. Designs can range from a central motif to pieces of varying width or length, stitched together in rows.

With most designs, you should aim for an even distribution of colors, tones (light or dark), and prints to create a balanced look. Where possible, avoid placing pieces of the same fabric side by side.

When cutting out the pieces, try to keep the grain of the fabric running in the same direction on each, ideally along the length. This looks better and helps prevent stretching, particularly on large pieces.

Piecing

Piecing means joining pieces together into larger and larger units. The method in most of the projects in this book is to pin the patches with right sides together and raw edges even, and then machine-stitch a straight seam. Use a medium stitch-length—about 12 stitches to 1 in. (2.5 cm)—removing the pins as you go. (If you wish, hand-baste the seams and remove the pins before machine-stitching them.)

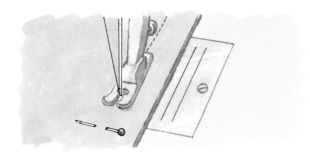

Seam allowances for piecing are ¼ in. (5 mm), which means you stitch exactly ¼ in. (5 mm) from the raw edges. Use the stitching guide on the machine if there is one; otherwise, use a separate magnetic gauge, a ¼-in. foot (patchwork foot), or a piece of tape as a guide. Keep the stitching as straight as possible. Press the seams open before stitching another seam across them.

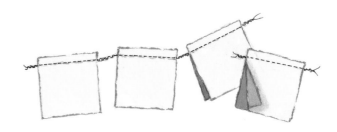

A quick way of stitching pieces together is to stitch them in a chain as shown, and then cut them apart later.

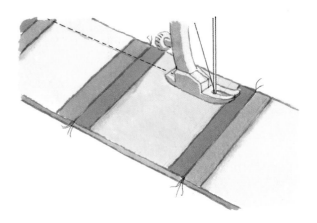

Pieces are often joined to form rows and the rows are then sewn together. If the pieces are all the same size, it's important to match the previously stitched seams. (If the seams don't match, restitch the seams that are too wide or narrow and unpick the old stitching before proceeding.) Make sure that the seam allowances are flat when you are stitching another seam across them.

In the projects in this book, seams are pressed open, but for extra strength they may be pressed to one side instead—to the darker side, where possible. For bulky fabrics, alternate seams should be pressed in the opposite direction.

A fast piecing method, known as strip-piecing, is to stitch strips rather than individual patches together, and then cut them at right angles to the seams to form new, pieced rows. Stitch the new rows together, staggering them or even flipping some of the rows around in order to vary the pattern. This method is especially useful if you want to incorporate a lot of small pieces.

Patchwork designs incorporating complicated shapes like pentagons, hexagons, and octagons have to be hand-sewn together, normally using backing papers, which are removed after the pieces are sewn together. Because it is more time-consuming than the machine-stitching technique, this type of patchwork is most suitable for small areas. The process is explained on pages 82–3.

Fabric paints

Widely available, fabric paints are a quick way of decorating a bag. Use a natural-fiber fabric such as cotton or silk, and be sure to experiment on scraps beforehand. You can paint the design on freehand, using a fine artist's brush, or apply it with a stamp and fabric paint. It's easiest to do this before sewing the bag, when the fabric can be laid flat and smooth. To fix the paint, place a piece of cotton over the design and iron it, following the paint manufacturer's instructions.

Quilting

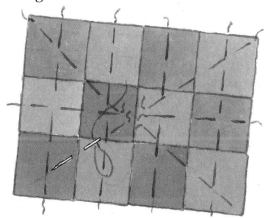

Quilting is the traditional partner to patchwork. Baste batting to the wrong side of the pieced fabric, using large running stitches as shown above. (For quilts, a backing fabric is traditionally placed behind the batting, but that isn't necessary here, because the bags will be lined.) Start at the center and work outward to the top and bottom, to each side, and to each corner.

To hand-quilt, place the fabric over the smaller ring of a quilting hoop, and push the larger ring over the top, adjusting the tightness with the screw. Now sew small, even running stitches or backstitches along the line of the pattern.

To machine-quilt, machine-stitch along the line of the pattern using a medium straight stitch.

Once the fabric is quilted, remove the basting.

Patterns can be based on any of the following approaches:
◆ "Stitch in the ditch," or "ditch-quilting," in which the quilting is in the seamlines of the patchwork.
◆ Quilting about ⅜ in. (1 cm) inside the seamline of each patch.
◆ An overall pattern, such as diamonds or curlicues, made after marking out the pattern on the right side of the fabric using a fade-away pen.
◆ A series of motifs, such as stars or flowers.

Hand embroidery

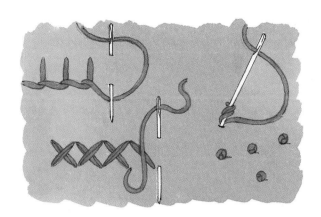

Embroidery can be used to add a wealth of detail to a bag. For the projects in this book, it is done prior to lining the bags. Shown above (clockwise from top left) are blanket stitch, French knot, and cross stitch.

Use stranded embroidery floss (separating the six strands and using just two or three, if you prefer), brilliant embroidery thread (also known as coton à broder), pearl cotton, matte embroidery thread, metallic thread, or an embroidery yarn. A hoop (see Special equipment, page 114) makes the process much easier but it is not essential.

Use a thread that is no longer than about 20 in. (50 cm), and weave the ends into the back rather than using knots.

Constructing a bag

Constructing a bag is fairly quick. The seams are stitched as described on page 116 under Piecing, except that, where possible, the seam allowances are ½ in. (1.5 cm), for extra strength. However, where this would affect the symmetry of the pieced design, the seam allowances are ¼ in. (5 mm), to match those of the piecing. To reinforce seams, especially at the base, you may wish to stitch again, alongside the first stitching, just within the seam allowance.

On curves, machine-stitch slowly and carefully, using smaller stitches. Keep the seam allowance even, avoiding any abrupt changes of direction. Curved seams will not lie flat unless you clip into the seam allowance (stopping just short of the stitching) at regular intervals after stitching. The greater the curve, the closer together they should be. For outward (convex) curves, cut slits. For inward (concave) curves, snip away wedge-shaped notches.

If the bag is flat, the front and back are stitched together at the sides and bottom in a continuous seam. When there are corners at the bottom, stop stitching once you are the width of the seam allowance from the edge. With the needle in the fabric, raise the presser foot and pivot the fabric to bring the new edge in line with the stitching guide. Lower the presser foot and continue stitching. Snip off the corners within the seam allowance to reduce bulk, turn right side out, and carefully push out the corners from inside.

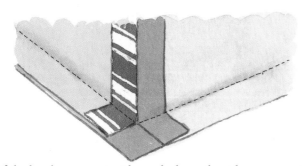

If the bag has separate sides and a base, the sides are sewn to the side edges of the front and back, and then the base is sewn to the bottom edges of the front, back, and sides. Each of the four side seams is left unstitched at the bottom by an amount equal to the width of the seam allowance, to allow the seam to open up around the corner.

Snap fasteners

 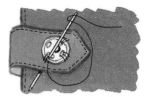

Many of the bags in this book are left open at the top, but some use closures, such as snaps. Snaps consist of a "ball," which is hand-sewn to the underside of an overlap, and a "socket," which is hand-sewn to the top side of an underlap, as shown above.

Zippers

A zipper is an effective way to close a bag but it is more noticeable than a snap. It must be applied early in the construction of the bag so that the fabric can be opened out flat while doing so. If possible, a zipper should be at least 2 in. (5 cm) shorter than the opening so that it is inserted into a seam. The seam allowance should be at least ½ in. (1.5 cm) wide, preferably wider for strength.

1 Mark points on the opening just beyond the top and bottom stops. If possible, stitch the seam on both sides of these points, even if it is just for an inch or so, then machine-baste the seam in between. Press it open and place the closed zipper face down over it on the wrong side. Pin and then hand-baste it in place down both sides and across both ends.

2 Put the zipper foot on the machine so it is to the left of the needle. With the zipper to the right of the needle, topstitch (machine-stitch from the right side) across one end, just outside the stop. Pivot at the corner and topstitch down the left side, about ¼ in. (5 mm) from the seam, as far as the other stop.

3 Pivot again, and topstitch across the end, just beyond the stop. Pivot, and topstitch down the other side ¼ in. (5 mm) from the seam until you are back at the start. Pull the top threads through to the wrong side and tie the threads. Remove the hand-basting on the zipper and the machine-basting along the seamline. Open the zipper.

Fabric handles and carriers

These are made in the same way as each other. If the ends will be hidden in the top seam of the bag, you can make them all as one long strip and then cut it into separate pieces. Otherwise, you will need to make them individually, as explained below. Use one of the following methods:

Use this method if you don't mind seeing the stitching or if the handle or carrier is quite narrow. Cut a strip for the carriers or fabric handles to four times the desired finished width, and the total finished length of all of them plus 1 in. (3 cm) per carrier or handle. This allows for ½-in. (1.5-cm) seam allowances at the ends. Fold the long edges into the center, wrong sides together. Press, and then fold in half lengthwise. Topstitch along this edge. Cut it into the required lengths.

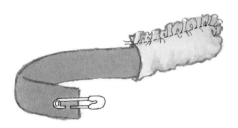

Use this method if you don't want the stitching to be visible and if the handle or carrier is not narrow. Cut the strip to twice the desired width, plus ½ in. (1 cm), and to the same length as above. Fold it in half lengthwise, right sides together, and stitch a ¼-in. (5 mm) seam along the long edge. Attach a safety pin to one end, and thread it through the tube, pulling the end of the tube with it, until it emerges at the other end. Pull it through, remove the safety pin, and press. Now cut it into the required lengths.

◆ If the ends of the handles or carriers will be visible on the finished bag, you can use either of the above methods but rather than one long strip at the beginning, you will need to cut individual strips, each the required finished length plus ½ in. (1 cm). In the first method, press under ¼ in. (5 mm) at each end before folding it in half. In the second method, stitch a ¼-in. (5 mm) seam across one end after stitching along the long edge; after turning it right side out, turn under ¼ in. (5 mm) seam allowances at the other end and slipstitch the opening.

Lining the bag

A lining creates a smooth interior and neatly finishes the top edge of the bag. You can use the same fabric as for the bag, or the same type of material but in a contrasting pattern or color. Purchased quilted fabric may also be used.

The lining is constructed in the same way as the bag, but without the piecing, decoration, or zipper. It is then attached to the top edge in one of the ways shown below, so that the bag and lining wind up wrong sides together.

If you want a really smooth fit, the lining can be ¼ in. (5 mm) narrower and ¼ in. (5 mm) shorter than the bag, but it would have to be attached by the first method shown below. However, for the projects in this book, the lining is always the same size as the bag.

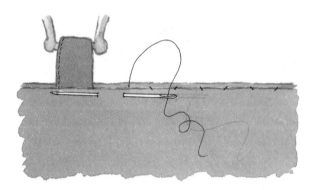

◆ In most of the projects, the top raw edges of the bag and lining are turned under by ½ in. (1.5 cm) and then simply stitched together either by machine or by hand. Machine-stitching will be visible, but hand-sewing will not if you use slipstitch, as shown above. (Any handles or carriers for handles are inserted into the seam from the top beforehand.)

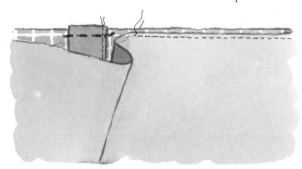

◆ An alternative method, used in some of the projects, is to leave the bottom seam of the lining unstitched and join the top edges of the lining and bag, right sides together and raw edges even. Then pull the lining up, press the seam, press under the seam allowances of the opening, and slipstitch the opening closed before tucking the lining inside. (Handles or carriers for handles are sandwiched in the top seam beforehand, with their ends even with the raw edges of the seam.)

templates

Photocopy or trace the template, enlarging it if it is not full-size. If it is one-third size, enlarge it to three times the size shown here; if it is one-half size, enlarge it to twice the size shown here. Cut out the shape and use this as a pattern to cut out the fabric.

Checkerboard Heart Bag (pp 24–7)

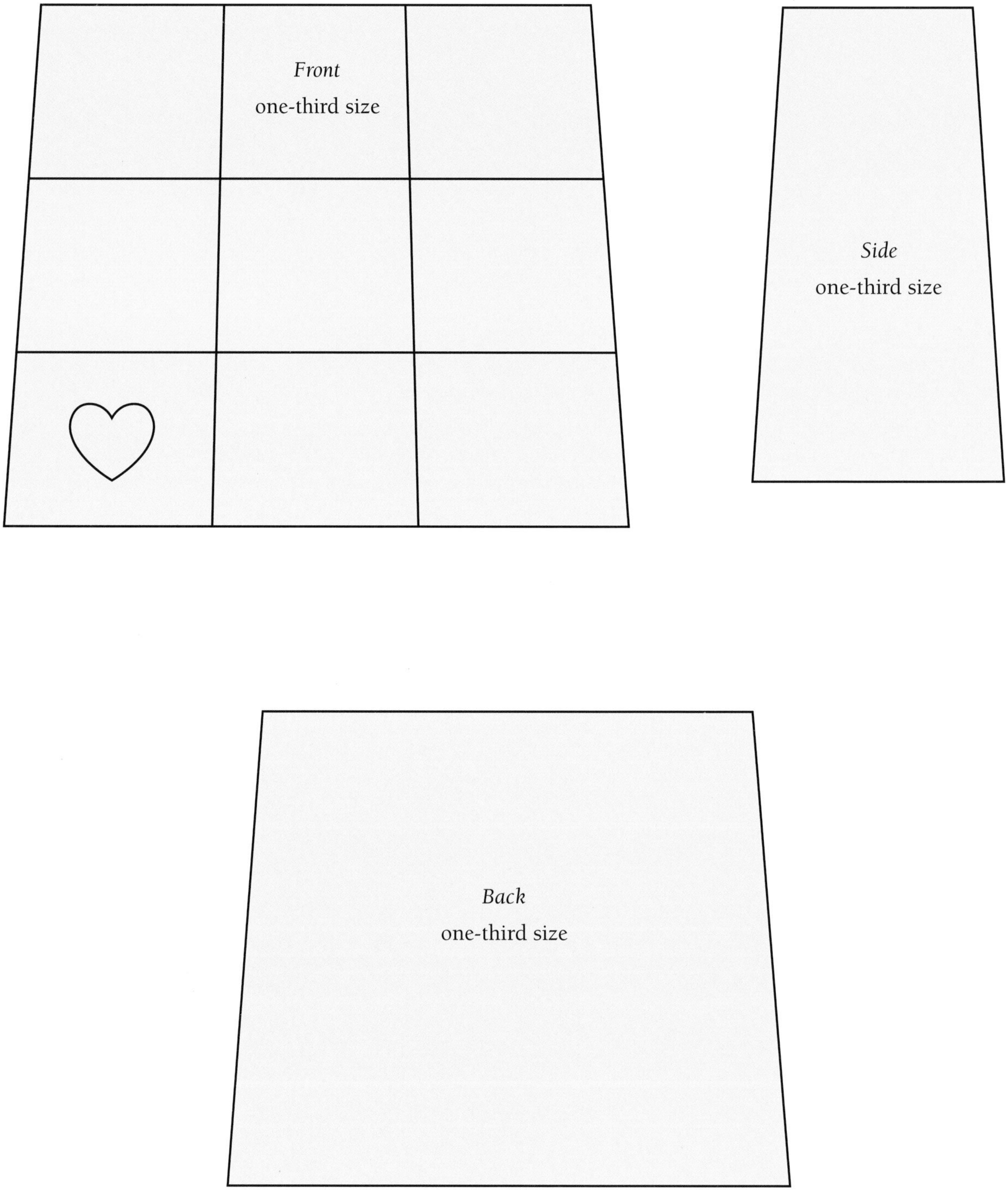

Front
one-third size

Side
one-third size

Back
one-third size

Summertime Tote (pp 38–41)

one-third size

Silk and Velvet Tote (pp 42–5)

one-third size

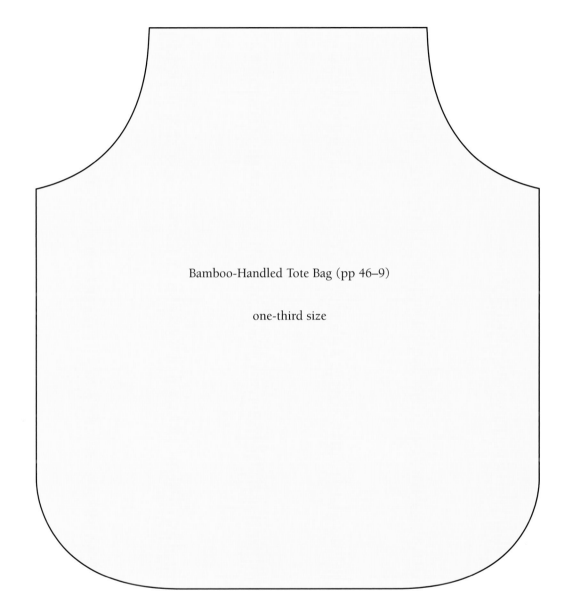

Bamboo-Handled Tote Bag (pp 46–9)

one-third size

Multicolored Tote (pp 50–3)

rectangles one-third size   flowers full-size

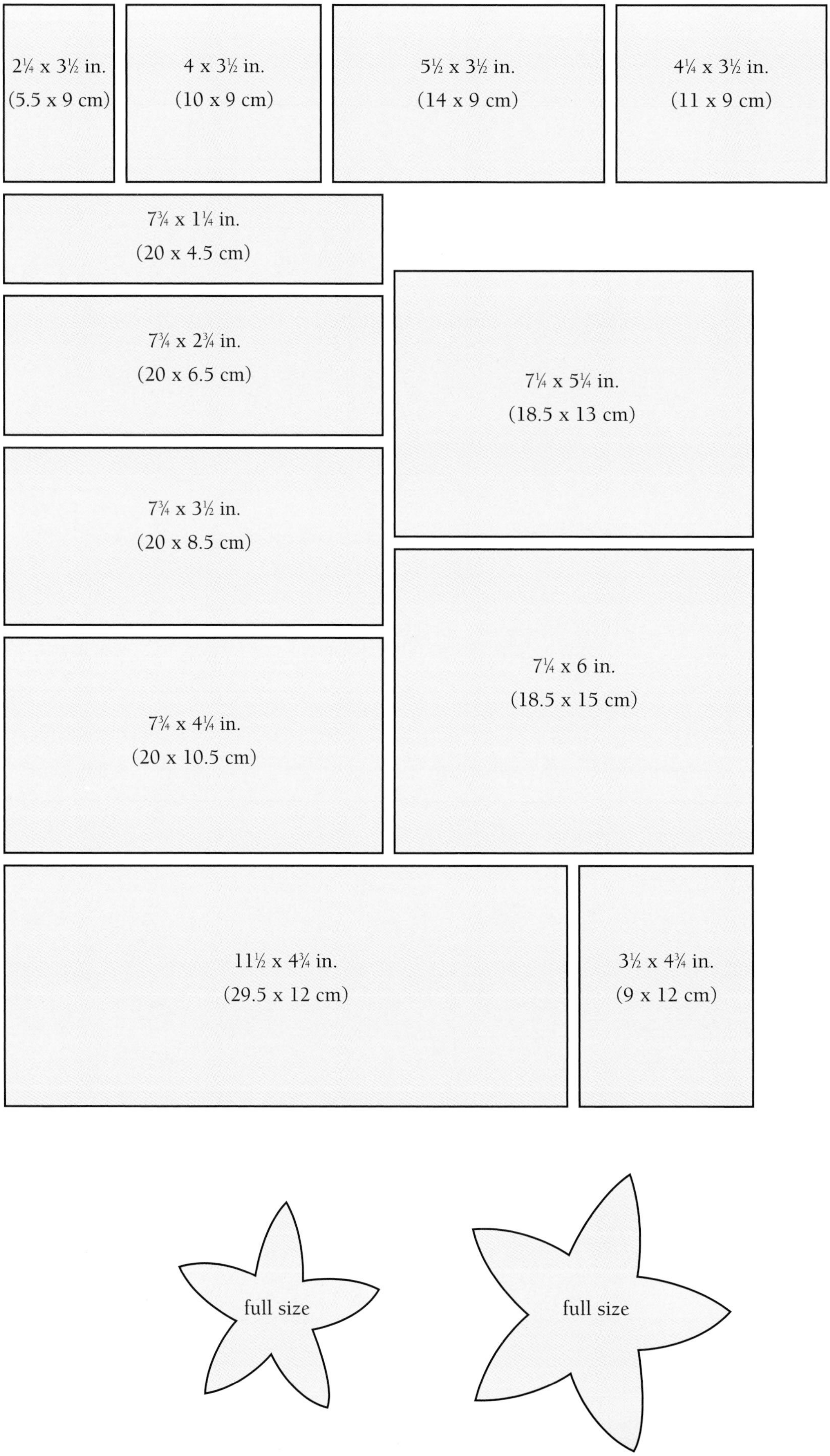

2¼ x 3½ in.
(5.5 x 9 cm)

4 x 3½ in.
(10 x 9 cm)

5½ x 3½ in.
(14 x 9 cm)

4¼ x 3½ in.
(11 x 9 cm)

7¾ x 1¼ in.
(20 x 4.5 cm)

7¾ x 2¾ in.
(20 x 6.5 cm)

7¼ x 5¼ in.
(18.5 x 13 cm)

7¾ x 3½ in.
(20 x 8.5 cm)

7¼ x 6 in.
(18.5 x 15 cm)

7¾ x 4¼ in.
(20 x 10.5 cm)

11½ x 4¾ in.
(29.5 x 12 cm)

3½ x 4¾ in.
(9 x 12 cm)

full size

full size

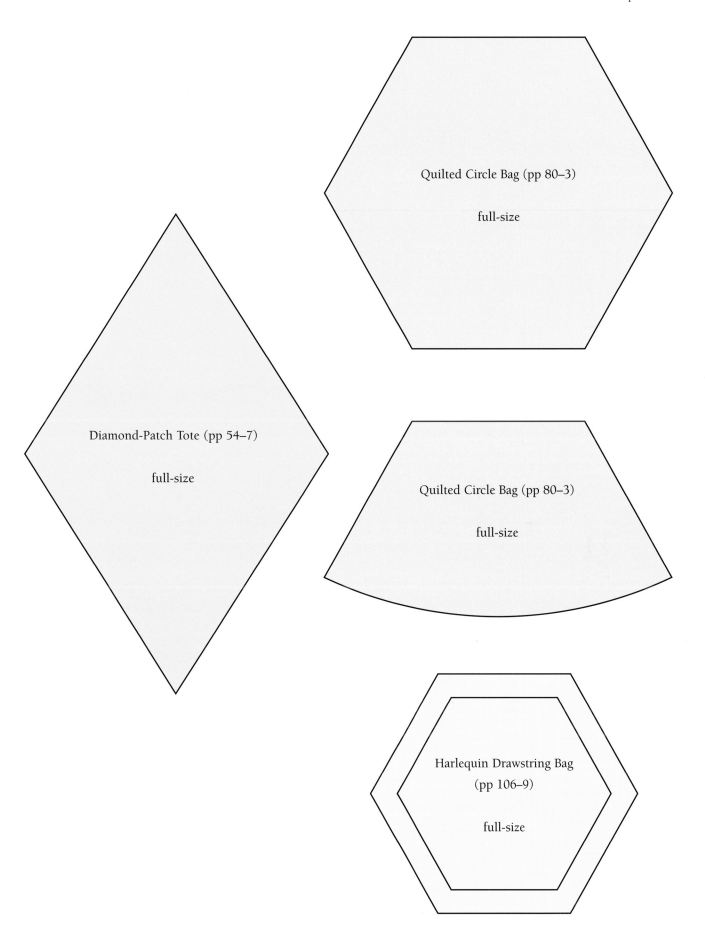

Quilted Circle Bag (pp 80–3)

full-size

Diamond-Patch Tote (pp 54–7)

full-size

Quilted Circle Bag (pp 80–3)

full-size

Harlequin Drawstring Bag
(pp 106–9)

full-size

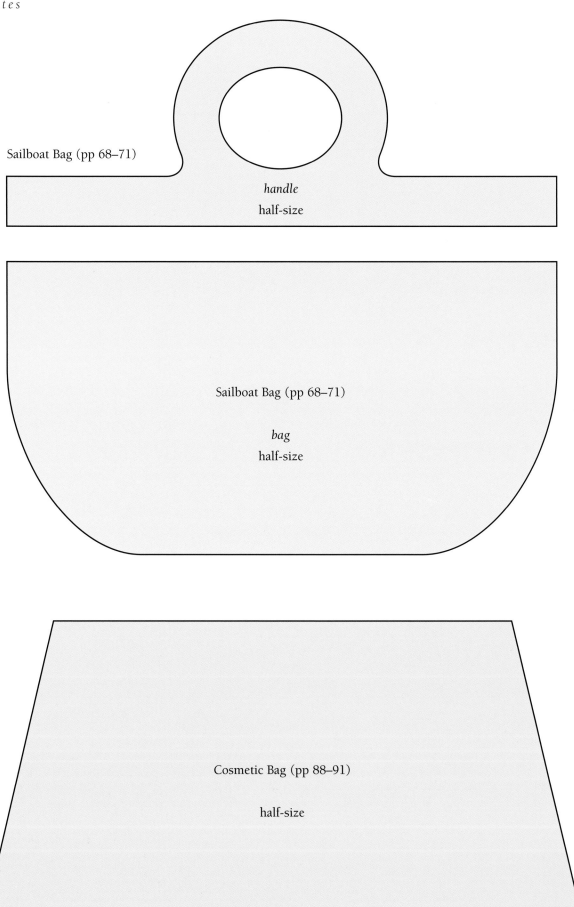

Sailboat Bag (pp 68–71)

handle
half-size

Sailboat Bag (pp 68–71)

bag
half-size

Cosmetic Bag (pp 88–91)

half-size

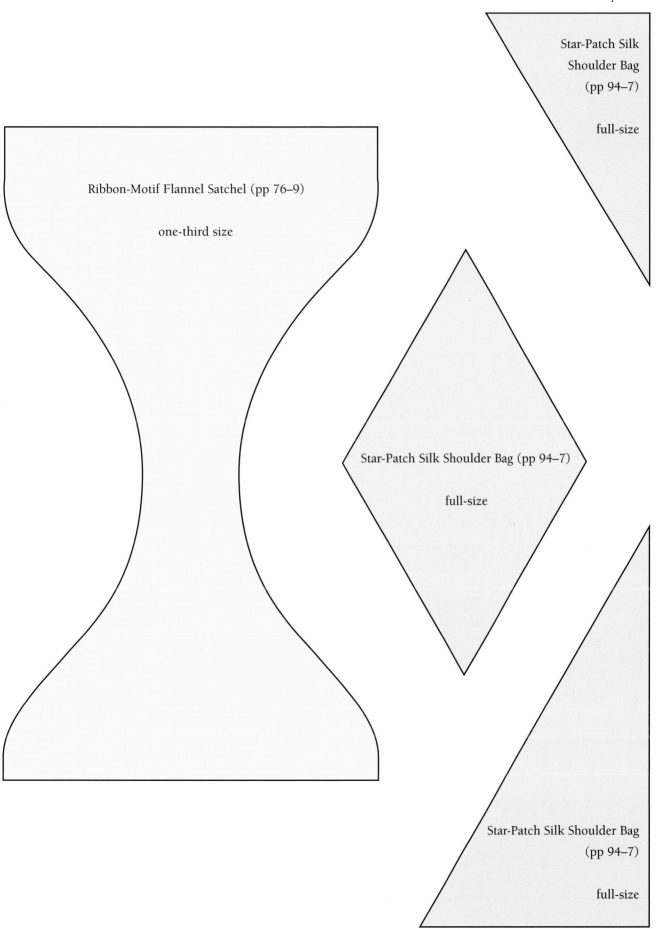

Star-Patch Silk
Shoulder Bag
(pp 94–7)

full-size

Ribbon-Motif Flannel Satchel (pp 76–9)

one-third size

Star-Patch Silk Shoulder Bag (pp 94–7)

full-size

Star-Patch Silk Shoulder Bag
(pp 94–7)

full-size

index